SEX AND SPIRIT

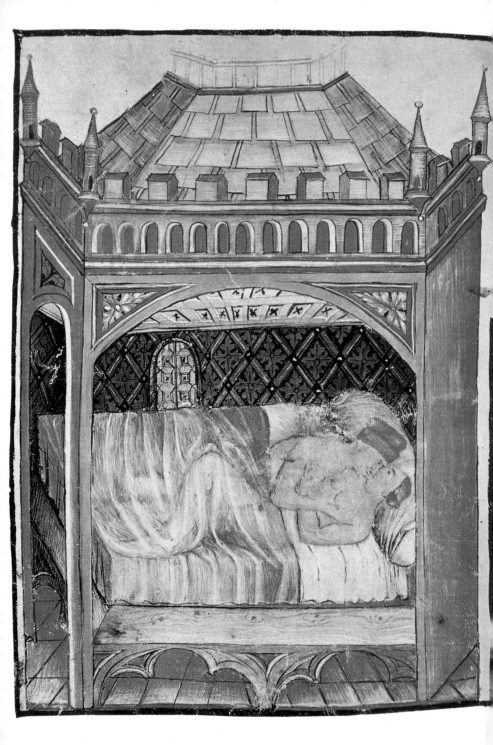

LIVING WISDOM

SEX AND SPIRIT

CLIFFORD BISHOP

SERIES CONSULTANT: **PIERS VITEBSKY**

MACMILLAN

IN ASSOCIATION WITH

DUNCAN BAIRD PUBLISHERS

Contents

Sex and Spirit

First published in Great Britain in 1996.

A DBP book
published by
Macmillan Reference Books
a division of Macmillan
Publishers Limited
25 Eccleston Place
London SW1W 9NF

A CIP catalogue record for this book is available from the British Library.

ISBN 0-333-67438-3

Conceived, created and designed by
Duncan Baird Publishers
Sixth Floor
Castle House
75–76 Wells Street
London W1P 3RE

10 9 8 7 6 5 4 3 2 1

Editor: Kirsty Seymour-Ure
Designer: Gabriella Le Grazie
with Sue Bush and Steve Painter
Design assistant: Richard Horsford
Picture research: Liz Eddison
Cartographic design: Line + Line

Typeset in Times NR MT.
Colour reproduction by
Colourscan, Singapore.
Printed in Singapore by
Imago Publishing Limited.

Introduction

The relationship between sex and spirit, body and mind, sensual appetites and transcendental aspirations, is a fundamental question whose resolution in different cultures reflects the multitude of ways in which human beings have struggled to make sense of themselves.

It is common for humans to conceive of the world as a sum of complementary pairs, such as good and evil, light and dark, male and female, body and soul. The most fundamental of these oppositions is that between subject and object – the knower and the known. Most people perceive themselves as discrete, bounded entities, able to experience the world around them but ultimately separate from it. This area of demarcation is felt as an inviolable sense of self, and is given many names: consciousness, ego, mind, soul – or spirit.

The writer Voltaire (1694–1778) asserted that "if God did not exist, it would be necessary to invent him", and the human mind has always projected its image onto the universe, and called the reflections demons, ghosts and gods. Through myth, religion and eventually science, the world was stamped in the shape of humanity, but even this did not stop the individual human self from feeling estranged; from being aware of what the 17th-century philosopher Blaise Pascal called the "immensity of spaces which I know not, and which know not me".

Throughout recorded history, and probably before, sex has been seen as a means – both physiological and symbolic – for healing this rupture between the human self and the rest of the universe. It has served as a physiological route to personal transcendence by acting as a form of intoxication. Nobody knows in detail how extreme pleasure "works", but it seems to activate some of the deepest and most primitive parts of the brain, occasionally over-riding the more complex, cognitive regions. Sexual ecstasy has widely been used, along with drugs, alcohol, music, dancing and breath-control techniques, as a way of dissolving the mind's sense of an exclusive self, and bringing about a union between different human spirits, or between a human spirit and that of a divinity, or divine essence. Sex has also been used to reunite humanity and the world symbolically, by associating the flow of reproductive energy through the human body with the flow of creative energy through the universe. Many societies perceive a link between human sexuality and plant and animal fertility and, by a form of sympathetic magic, ritualized sex becomes a society's guarantor of its own success and the fruitfulness of the earth.

Sexual conduct has always, therefore, been too important to be left to individual discretion. Historically, the complex of rituals, myths, taboos and edicts surrounding sex has been a large part of how people have organized themselves in relation to each other, to their environment and to their gods. All religions legislate for the power of sex, whether by restraining it via monasticism and chastity, or by licensing it through orgiastic and ritual outlets. It has even been suggested that religion, art and culture – all things typically thought of as a manifestation of the human spirit – are actually sublimations of the sex drive. This book examines the history and practice of all these different relationships between sex and the human spirit.

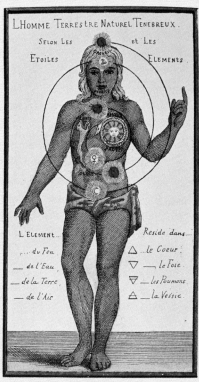

Both Eastern and Western mystical traditions have a history of portraying the universe in human form and, simultaneously, the human body as a microcosm of the universe. This engraving of the cosmic spiral within the body of man, from J.G. Gritchel's Theosophica Practice *(1898), shows the body containing four elements – earth, air, fire and water – making a clear link between the characteristics of humans and those of the universe.*

Origins

The beliefs, and most of the practices, of prehistoric humans can only be guessed at, based on a miscellany of paintings, bones, artefacts and carvings. Although we can never know exactly how paleolithic and early neolithic people thought, the surviving evidence suggests a profound and widespread association between human sexuality and the abundance of game animals on which life depended. A similar link can be found in the traditional hunting societies that still survive. The idea that human sexual behaviour influences the well-being of the cosmos and the fertility of the earth also finds expression in the earliest-known texts – those from ancient Sumer – and in the rituals of agricultural communities worldwide. Private, intimate acts become the subject of social control – through some magical sympathy, they are held to affect the whole of society, by changing the physical world.

An illustration from an 11th-century manuscript showing the goddess of the earth as Nature arising from the ground. The image of a woman suckling animals reveals the vestiges of a profound sense of the link between humans and the rest of the natural world.

The invention of marriage

Marriage – in all its forms, from monogamy to structured polygamy – is not, strictly speaking, natural to humans. It had to be invented, and thus is one of the first acts by which humans started to shape themselves, rather than be shaped by nature.

Early humans are thought to have evolved from chimp-like creatures. They formed social groups in which a dominant male tried to ensure exclusive sexual access to a large number of females, in order to increase his chances of finding a female on heat and of passing on his genes to future generations. At the same time, the females would try to mate with a series of younger, more fertile males. There would have been nothing resembling a pair bond in these early groups. This pattern of behaviour resembles some forms of harem-based polygyny (one man with several wives), although even in most nominally polygynous societies, monogamy has in fact been the social norm.

The invention of marriage may be the triumph of the imagination over the physical, but it probably would not have occurred without certain evolutionary changes in the body. The most important of these was the development away from the oestrus cycle, in which females are only periodically on heat. A male is far more likely to be satisfied with one female if that female is permanently sexually receptive, as humans are. It is surely no coincidence that the only other monogamous primates are gibbons – also not subject to an oestrus cycle.

Most cultures traditionally see marriage as the basis of society, and separate it rigorously from the destabilizing influences of love and passion (see pp. 112–13). Perhaps the only recorded society with no form of marriage has been the Nayar of the Malabar coast of India. Until the 19th century, Nayar girls underwent an initiation rite before the onset of menstruation. Each girl was

ABOVE *A Bronze Age rock-painting of a wedding ceremony, from Bohuslan, Sweden. The legs are tied as in a modern Romany wedding.* RIGHT *This wooden carving, made by the Senufo of West Africa, depicts a primordial couple. Human marriage patterns were often supposedly in imitation of the marriage of the gods.*

MARRIAGE PAYMENTS

The world has traditionally been divided into those cultures that insist on a bride-wealth payment from the husband to the bride or her parents, and those that insist on a dowry (by which the bride or her parents in effect purchase a husband). The nature of the marriage payment seems to depend on whether it is considered more shameful in that culture for a mature man or for a mature woman to go unmarried. In ancient Lydia, according to the 5th-century BC Greek historian Herodotus, there was so much pressure for women to marry that they earned their own dowries by prostitution. In dowry cultures, female babies tend to be valued less than male, and may even be killed at birth.

By contrast, in bride-wealth cultures, daughters are prized as financial assets – although this does mean that they may have little more status than any other kind of

A couple depicted on an Egyptian stone tablet (presumed 1980–1640BC). Property in ancient Egypt often passed through the female line.

property. In ancient Assyria, young unmarried women belonged to the state, which auctioned them off to the highest bidder, and a man was obliged to marry the woman he bought. The Assyrians were so keen to see their women married that they combined bride-wealth with dowry. After most of the women had been sold, a part of the profits was put aside as bait to find husbands for those remaining, each of whom was put up for "auction" and given to the man prepared to accept her with the least sum of money. At an Indonesian Weyewa marriage, the husband compensates the bride's family with "male" gifts such as cattle and gold, while the bride takes with her a dowry of "female" objects such as pigs and cloth. The extensive nature of these exchanges means that divorce is extremely rare, as it is impossible to unravel the distribution of gifts.

secluded with an adult male sponsor, who deflowered her. The sponsor might later become her lover, and she and her children had to perform mourning taboos on his death, but aside from this, they had no claims on him nor he on them. At the other extreme, the Nyinbar of Nepal tolerate many forms of marriage, including polygyny, polyandry (one woman with several husbands, usually brothers) and conjoint marriages in which a polyandrously married man takes an extra wife. But polyandry is the preferred form, and through modern folklore and legends of polyandrous ancestors, it is the way in which the Nyinbar define themselves as a culture.

Marriage solves some uniquely human problems. For example, children must be looked after for much longer than the young of other animals, and a lasting bond between parents is one way of achieving this. After early humans learned to hunt, this bond had to be able to survive long periods of separation. Nevertheless, cultures throughout history have had to offer incentives or apply penalties to make their members (usually the men) accede to marriage. Bachelors in ancient Sparta were dragged around an altar and beaten by young women, or forced to run naked through the streets in winter, singing songs that ridiculed their single state.

Woman, man and beast

The idea of the hunt as a form of sexual union can be found wherever humans rely on game animals for their survival. Hunting cultures are highly aware that their own substance comes from the flesh of another, once living, being. The life of the animal they have killed has now become their own life, and they identify strongly with what they chase and destroy. In the myths of hunting cultures, knowledge and power (or even humanity itself) will often have come from animals. These gifts will have been granted, and may still be channelled, by sexual means, and the animals concerned will be spoken of as ancestors.

According to one 20th-century Athabascan hunter of the North American Pacific coast: "We know what the animals do, what are the needs of the beavers, the bear, the salmon and other creatures, because long ago men married them and acquired this knowledge from their animal wives." Some Athabascan groups relate that in the time before humans married the animals and gained their medicine, their roles were reversed, and humans were hunted by giant predecessors of the

Leda and the Swan, *attributed to Nicolas Poussin (1594–1665). The ancestral spirit-animal may survive into the so-called high cultures in the myths of gods that assume animal shape, in order to rape or seduce human women. The offspring may be heroic, as in the case of Castor and Polydeuces (Pollux), born after Leda's rape by Zeus in the form of a swan; or they may be monstrous, as in the case of the Minotaur, conceived when Pasiphaë, wife of King Minos, hid herself in an artificial cow to tempt a bull sent by Poseidon, the god of the sea.*

HUNTERS AND FERTILITY

The presence of a great many cave-paintings of animals in deep, womb-like caves may be interpreted as a form of fertility magic, intended to promote the birth of more game animals from the womb of the earth. The association of human with animal fertility is suggested by sites such as Pech-Merle, France, with its wall-paintings showing human and animal–human coitus side by side.

The paleolithic hunter's concern with fertility is also suggested by the discovery of numerous stone "Venuses", or figurines with exaggerated secondary sexual characteristics. The preponderance of these figures has led to speculation that paleolithic communities were matriarchal or possibly even vagina-worshipping, and that women were seen as the sole source of human life, because paleolithic people were ignorant of the male role in

The Venus of Willendorf, dating from c.30,000–25,000BC, is a personification of fecundity.

conception (see pp.40–45). This matriarchal age was brought to an end by agrarian and nomadic peoples who had developed a firmer understanding of biology.

Nevertheless, a hunting culture did not always mean a matriarchal culture; neither did a reverence for female icons necessarily translate into a powerful social position for women, as evidenced by the relatively low status of women in many Catholic countries, in which the Virgin Mary is revered. The holy temple to the fertility goddess Demeter, at Eleusis, was destroyed only in AD410, long after Greece had become a male-dominated culture. Present-day hunting cultures, such as those of Siberia and Alaska, are not appreciably matriarchal.

beaver and other creatures. Similarly, the Mandan of the North American Plains – whose survival depended on the bison and whose way of life was wiped out along with the great herds – thought that human society was descended from a sexual transfer of power between a bison and a woman. The Buffalo Dance, an ancient ritual which, according to tradition, existed before the Mandan developed tools or social organization, mirrored this primordial act. The dance was to ensure abundant bison herds. A respected matron engaged in sexual intercourse with a man of power, who carried a "medicine bundle" (an object believed to be a source of spirit power), and represented the bison. In the dance, the woman mimed the act of extracting power from the bundle-carrier.

This manifest flow of life from the hunted to the hunter suggests that there is a limited supply of life energy – there

Antelope-headed dancers from Mali perform a dance to celebrate the ancestral animal spirits.

In some New Guinea dance rituals (right), a man dresses as a bird of paradise: the incarnation of a beautiful young spirit woman. The watching men remark lasciviously on the beauty of the dancer, and express their sexual frustration as they flirt with each other. An accumulation of such frustration would be channelled into energy for the hunt.

HUMAN QUARRY

If the hunting of animals has often and widely been likened to a seduction or a marriage, then seduction has equally often been compared to the hunt. Some 19th-century neo-Darwinists, such as J.F. McLennan and Lord Avebury, even suggested that the forcible capture of women from neighbouring groups was the prototypical way in which primitive men

Maenads, feral women who hunted and sacrificed men with their bare hands, could themselves become the object of erotic pursuit, as shown on this 2nd-century BC Greek vase.

obtained wives. The near-universal human prohibitions against incest were claimed to have arisen from this practice of marrying outside a clan or kinship group (see pp.120–23).

There is very little evidence to support this belief. The example usually quoted was Columbus's description of the native Caribbeans, who "make descents on other islands, where they capture all the women they can get hold of". However, Columbus added that, "these they keep in their service and as concubines" – not as wives. In addition, Carib marriage rules prescribed a rigid system of cross-cousin marriage (that is, within the group). Spanish missionaries in the Amazon Basin – where the abduction of women became the chief object of warfare among some peoples – also described the captives being kept as slaves, rather than as wives. Women taken in warfare throughout the Americas have usually been handed to the women of the captors' own tribe to help with their work. The Navajo were said to steal Ute women specifically to obtain skilled basket-makers.

On the other hand, elopement or the mock-abduction of a woman is a common custom in African marriage, undertaken only after arrangements have been made with the bride's family. Traditionally, a Kenyan Waitata woman would be carried off shrieking by her husband and four friends, followed by a jeering crowd of girls. The Tikopia of Polynesia practised bride-capture until the 1920s, according to elaborate codes of etiquette.

are only so many souls, endlessly recycled. Holy men or shamans may have to visit a spirit master or mistress of animals, to bargain for the number of animal souls their people may hunt. Sometimes, as with the Desana of Colombia, they have to offer human souls in trade. In consequence, Desana couples are discouraged from having too many children, as this uses up the available life energy. In the native communities of the Bering Sea and eastern Greenland, barren women may believe that the reason they have not conceived is that there is a shortage of souls waiting to be born. These women ask shamans to hunt down an unclaimed soul for them, so they may have a baby.

A Desana hunt is a form of courtship. As among hunting peoples worldwide, it is preceded by a period of sexual abstinence – of at least one day, during which the man must not even have an erotic dream – to produce a state of sexual excitement and a powerful latent charge of sexual energy. As part of his preparation for the hunt, a Desana man must wash and purify himself and his

weapons, after which he may apply perfumes made from aromatic herbs, which arouse the animal that he is hunting and lure it to him. The Desana verb for "to hunt" translates as "to make love to the animals". The penetration of the animal's body with an arrow is analogous to sexual penetration, and the hunter always pays particular attention to the dead animal's genitalia, commenting on their size and shape. The erotic relationship between animals and Desana men extends into their dreams, in which an animal will present itself willingly to a man to be fertilized, in order to multiply its own species.

In Siberia, game animals may be encouraged to multiply, by means of sexually explicit dances. These are performed communally, as part of a "renewal of life" ceremony, and imitate the rutting of elk and reindeer. A Siberian shaman may also perform a solo rutting dance to represent sexual union with the sister or the daughter of the master of animals, an act that gives him extra leverage when negotiating for prey for his community.

A Mayan painted dish from Guatemala (AD 675–750) depicting a woman being fondled by spider monkeys, symbols of sexual excitement. Animal spirits are frequently accused of becoming incubi or succubi, copulating with humans, usually in dreams, to steal their vital energy. In Borneo, monkeys may take on the shape of a woman's husband in order to lie with her. The Chinese fox is a demon who is able to take the form of a beautiful man or woman. Among the Colombian Desana, men are accustomed to dreaming about sex with animals – so those creatures who wish to absorb a man's energy do not even need to assume a human shape.

The fertile earth

Humans tend to see their own activities and motives written large in the forces of nature. Even when natural phenomena are not given names, personalities and associated dramas, as they are in most early religions, they are often seen as behaving in a recognizably human manner. Thus, the fertility of the earth appears inextricably linked to the fertility, and by extension the sexual customs, of humans.

For the Mongols and the early Chinese, the sky fertilized the earth by sending down its seed in the form of rain. Similar beliefs survive in parts of Africa and Australia, where women who wish to conceive may go out and lie in a rainstorm; and the first women of the Trobriand Islands, Papua New Guinea, are said to have exposed their vaginas to the rain, so that they would be opened and spirits could enter them to make children (see pp.40–45).

The oldest recorded hymn comes from Sumer in the 3rd millennium BC. In it, the goddess Inanna (forerunner of the Babylonian Ishtar, who as the morning star was eternally virgin, but as the evening star was "the divine harlot") asks, "Who will plough my vulva? Who will plough my high field? Who will plough my wet ground?" She is answered by Dumuzzi, her brother (or sometimes her son) and lover, "Great lady, the king will plough your vulva. I, Dumuzzi the king, will plough your

MOTHERHOOD AND PRIESTHOOD

Except in cases of male physical impotence – which is itself often blamed on women's witchcraft – a childless marriage has usually been considered the fault of the woman. Gods and goddesses (and the Virgin Mary) are still regularly petitioned for personal fertility. Earth goddesses, with their yearly cycles, have been less popular for this purpose than moon goddesses – such as the Greek Artemis, or the Roman Lucina – whose cycles seem more clearly linked to a woman's own. Ithyphallic (perpetually aroused) gods, such as the Indian Gopalsami, are also often invoked to make a woman fertile, and phallic emblems are among the most common fertility charms.

One cure for barren women is to be impregnated by a priest or holy man who is considered to have been deputized by the gods. The Jewish historian and theologian Josephus (c.AD37–c.100) claimed that a man named Decius Mundus played the role of the jackal-headed god Anubis in one temple to Isis, and impregnated any women who came asking the goddess to help them conceive. Several accounts from between the 16th and the 19th centuries tell of Indian fakirs who were begged to bestow their favours in the street, while in the 18th century, the church of Orcival in Auverge, France, had a canon who was legendary in the district as "the pillar which makes women fruitful".

A marble statue depicting the multibreasted Artemis of the Ephesians, dating from the 2nd century AD. Artemis was a fertility goddess and guardian of childbirth, and at the same time a virgin huntress. An explanation of this strange conjunction is that the Artemis of the Ephesians was an early deity whose attributes were grafted on to a later goddess – although the psychologist Carl Jung believed virginity to be a characteristic of the archetypal mother goddess (see pp.108–9).

vulva." The heavenly congress of the god and goddess was thought to guarantee the fertility of the earth, so the Sumerians, through their rituals, had to ensure that such congress took place. At harvest time, the union of Inanna and Dumuzzi was re-enacted by a priestess and the king, who, for that moment, became incarnations of the divine couple, waking them from the timelessness of myth and making them active in the everyday world.

It is impossible to say how long this practice of mystical marriage, widely known by its Greek name of *hieros gamos*, had existed even before the Sumerians, but the earliest examples of male and female divinities represented as couples occur in the shrines of Çatal Hüyük in Anatolia (*c*.6000BC).

The idea of the *hieros gamos* was central to the mystery cult of Demeter, the goddess of agriculture, which originated in antiquity at Eleusis near Athens and survived until AD389, when it was suppressed by the Christian emperor Theodosius I. Only fragmentary descriptions of the Eleusinian mysteries (secret rituals) survive. It seems that there was a lesser mystery, celebrated in February, miming the abduction of Demeter's daughter Persephone, by Hades, lord of death. In mourning for her lost daughter, Demeter condemned the earth to be barren. The greater mystery was performed in September, in the sacred

A detail from a Greek vase from 430–420BC, showing a woman watering phalluses that are set into the ground. The phalluses are likely to have been made of terracotta: such models were common votive offerings at certain shrines. In ancient Greece, phallic symbols were thought to promote fertility, especially in cults that were devoted to the worship of the god Dionysos or his son, the ithyphallic Priapus.

temple of initiation, and celebrated the return of Persephone and the resultant fruiting
of the earth. At its climax, the
hierophant (priest) produced an
ear of corn, and announced,
"The Terrible One has given
birth to the Terrible One". The
ear of corn not only symbolized,
but was, the child that Perse-

*A wooden deblé or rhythm pounder,
used by the Senufo people of West
Africa, who pound the earth during
rituals to promote the fertility of the soil.*

phone bore to Hades – a son born to
death, which made death the creator of
life and the saviour of humanity. After
the revelation of the ear of corn, a
sacred marriage took place between the
hierophant and the priestess of Demeter
to ensure the next year's mystery. The
spirit of the *hieros gamos* still survives in
some European spring festivals: on
these occasions a young man is chosen
to be the May king, Green Man or king
of the Green – embodying the idea of
new life from death – and is symbolically married to a young woman, the
queen of the May.

MYTHS OF DEATH AND LIFE

In Sumerian myth, after the death of her lover,
the goddess Inanna descends to the underworld to attend his funeral. There she is
stripped, turned into a corpse and hung from a
hook in the wall, by her elder sister Erishkigal,
queen of the underworld. But after three days
and nights, the goddess rises again and returns
to the sky as the first being ever to return from
the kingdom of the dead. Her story is the
prototype for those of Ishtar and Tammuz, Isis
and Osiris, Demeter and Persephone and all
the other goddesses who must redeem their
lovers or children (or both) from death so that
the life of the earth itself can continue. The
period when the goddess is in the underworld
(or, with Isis, wandering in the wilderness) is
the barren season, when no crops grow.

Similar myths were re-enacted well into the
19th century by the Shilluk and other peoples
of the Sudan, in acts of periodic regicide. The
body of the king would be buried beside a
living virgin girl, and when the bodies were
decomposed, their bones would be gathered in
the hide of a bull and re-buried. A year later a
new king would be chosen, and his reign would
begin with the lighting of a holy fire by a virgin
boy and girl, who would then perform their
own first copulation together before being
thrown into a pit and buried alive.

*A late 6th-century BC Etruscan tomb painting
showing Ceres (the Roman form of Demeter)
carrying an ear of corn. Agricultural motifs were
central to the cult of Demeter, who was believed
to protect the bounty of the earth and the crops.*

Among the Native Americans of the San Juan Pueblo, New Mexico, the Deer Dance is performed to ensure bounteous crops, rather than more deer.

HUNTERS AND FARMERS

Some agricultural fertility rituals possess elements that have survived from the hunting/gathering past of a people. The Blackfoot Native Americans perform a ritual dance in which a man decks himself with feathers and imitates the mating display of a prairie cock; the intention is to ensure a good crop of corn.

The symbolic marriage of animals and humans (see pp.12–15) commonly found in hunting societies is transformed into an agricultural fertility rite in the horse sacrifice described in the Indian Rig Veda (written *c*.1400BC). A specially selected horse was released by the king to wander freely for a year, after which time it was caught, tied to a sacrificial post and smothered. The wife of the king then lay with the horse's corpse and mimed intercourse with it, while the officiating priests exchanged ritually prescribed obscenities. The queen represented the "field", or earth, which was "ploughed" by the horse and fructified by his seed, which was thought to come from the sun.

ABSTINENCE

Just as some cultures have believed that the expenditure of sexual energy could inspire a similar activity in nature, others act as though human sexual activity might, conversely, contaminate the reproduction of the crops, or as though human abstinence will build up a store of excess sexual energy that the earth needs in order to be properly fruitful. For example, if a couple from the Akan of Ghana have sex outside on the ground, the offended earth goddess Asase Yaa will strike them down with madness and make the ground where they lay infertile. In regions as far apart as Nicaragua and Transylvania it is a folk custom that a man may not sleep with his wife during the time in which he is sowing crops.

Virginity and defloration

The loss of virginity is seen as a form of initiation – a change in the fundamental nature of one's being – in even the most modern, secularized societies. In many religious codes it represents an irreversible fall from a state of perfection. The virgin is unspoiled, still full of potential and, crucially in the case of a girl, whole or unbroken. North American Blackfoot girls announced their virtue publicly by claiming the right to cut up the perfect bison tongues which were used in the sacred Sun Dance. The Blackfoot placed a high value on chastity, and the girl would have to proclaim the names of men whose advances she had fought off, in the way that warriors announced their coups.

While the virginity of a boy is usually a matter of trust or hearsay, that of a girl is assumed to be demonstrable (although there are many ways in which a girl may accidentally lose her physical virginity, and there are techniques dating back to ancient Egypt for faking virginal haemorrhage). Because the demonstration involves the spilling of blood, itself a ritually significant act, it is usually only the virginity – and defloration – of women that has been transformed into public rite and spectacle.

Women have been widely considered blessed if they have their first congress with a god, or with one of a god's deputies such as a holy man or a king. Ritual defloration may also involve an element of sympathetic magic, designed to increase the fertility of people, lands and livestock. Any sacrifice to a god usually consists of the first or choicest portion: the first crops, the first lambs, even the first-born child of a family. The literal sacrifice of a virgin – as in ancient Thebes, where the most beautiful and aristocratically born virgin girl would be sacrificed each year to Zeus – often became transmuted to a symbolic sacrifice of her virginity. St Augustine (AD354–430) described a Roman statue of Priapus "upon whose huge and beastly member the new bride was commanded ... to sit". The 4th-century AD writer Lactantius described the same deity, "in whose shameful lap brides sit, in order that the god

VESTAL VIRGINS

Vesta was a Roman goddess of the hearth, tended by virgins because she was, as Ovid writes, "naught but the living flame, and ... no bodies are born of flame. Rightly ... is she a virgin who neither gives nor takes seeds, and she loves companions in her virginity." Her sacred fire was tended by six priestesses, the Vestal Virgins, to ensure her goodwill toward the Roman state. When Rome suffered a military fiasco at Cannae in 216BC, the blame fell not on the army, but on two Vestals who were accused of failing in their ritual duties. Vestal Virgins were selected between the ages of six and ten from aristocratic families by the high priest of Vesta. Their vows committed them to chastity for the next thirty years, after which they could marry. A Vestal who surrendered her virginity was buried alive.

A Vestal Virgin from the House of the Vestals in the Roman Forum.

The Annunciation *(1438–45) by Fra Angelico: the angel relays to Mary the news that, despite her virgin state, she is to bear the child of God.*

VIRGIN BIRTHS

At the temple to Aphrodite in Paphos, Cyprus, the women of the city had to prostitute themselves once to a stranger before they could marry. But they were still considered virgins, and any children born as a result were termed "born of a virgin", and raised in the temple.

Pagan gods and human leaders, heroes or sages – including Alexander the Great, Plato and Julius Caesar – were often claimed to be the offspring of a virgin birth. Early Christian writers felt they had to explain away the births of gods such as Dionysos (born from the thigh of Zeus): commentators from the theologian Origen in the 3rd century to Cardinal Newman in the 19th have interpreted pagan virgin births as God's way of preparing the world for the birth of Christ. The Virgin Birth was widely ridiculed in the early days of Christianity, not because it was implausible but because virgin birth was so common. There were rumours that Jesus was the son of a Roman centurion, Pantherus, or even that Mary had incestuously conceived with her brother. With the doctrine of the Immaculate Conception, Mary herself was claimed to have been born of a virgin, and thus to be free of the taint of original sin.

Yali men of western Papua New Guinea arrive in traditional dress, with bows and arrows, for their pig-killing ceremony. This ceremony resembles a mythical tradition that can be traced back to ancient Greece, where the pig was one of the representations of the virgin Kore (Persephone). The killing of the pig is a symbolic spilling of virginal blood as a sacrifice to ensure the fecundity of nature.

may have gathered the first fruits of their virginity".

The most common reason for ritual defloration, found worldwide but best documented in Asia, is to remove from the husband the duty of breaking his wife's hymen and being contaminated with her blood. In certain cultures, all blood is either unclean or charged with a transformative power. Often, little distinction is made between blood from a virginal haemorrhage and menstrual blood, which is taboo (see pp.124–5).

DEFINITIONS OF VIRGINITY

Historical and cross-cultural accounts of virginity are complicated by problems of translation. Not everyone has the same definition of what constitutes a virgin. For example, a widow in the Trobriand Islands, after a period of mourning, once more becomes a virgin (or "one filled with vitality"). The Romans (and the Greeks before them) differentiated between a woman who was merely *virgo*, or unmarried and therefore independent, and one who was actually *virgo intacta* (untouched). It is possible that modern accounts of ancient virgin births are based on similar confusions.

According to the sacred Indian texts, the Vedas, the blood flowing from first intercourse has in it a poison which is the root of all evils. Among the Canelos of India, it is thought that an evil spirit called Supai rises from the first blood of intercourse and tries to harm the husband because it loves the bride and is determined to have her for itself. Such malign forces are best confronted by a god, priest or man of power.

In 13th-century Cambodia, the daughter of a wealthy family was deflowered between the ages of seven and nine by a Buddhist priest, who received gifts of wine, cloth or silver. A priest could deflower one virgin a year. Sometimes the priest and virgin did not actually copulate: he might take her virginity with his finger, then dip his finger into wine, which was sprinkled on the heads of relatives and neighbours as a sacrament. In Thailand in the 15th century, a priest would go with a bridegroom to the bride's house, where he would "tear off the red of the maiden and sprinkle the bridegroom's forehead with it".

In the early 20th century, among the Muslims of Chinese Turkestan, it was a common practice for families to invite the *akhund* (priest) to deflower their ten-year-old daughters. This ceremony was known as "opening the closed", and was performed without any medical precautions. So many girls were disabled through infection that the governor of the Hsin-chiang province outlawed the ceremony on girls younger than fourteen; but without it, no man would take a girl for his wife.

Priests are not the only people to perform ritual deflorations. On the principle that like cannot pollute like, virgin girls may be deflowered by women, as occurs among the Bantu Paia of Africa. A king might have not merely the opportunity but the obligation to lie with a bride before handing her to her husband, and King Conchobar of ancient Ireland was highly praised for his devotion to duty in this regard. The tradition led to the *jus primae noctis*, or *droit de seigneur*, of medieval Europe, in which a feudal lord could claim the right to sleep with a woman on her wedding night. From Tibet to New Guinea, travellers and strangers arriving in a village often found themselves presented with virgins for the night. As outsiders, they were considered either immune to contamination from the blood, or not worth worrying about; and any evil they released, they took away with them.

The tradition of freeing a man from the sole risk and responsibility of taking his bride's virginity can also be found in the so-called Nasamonian custom (first attributed by the 5th-century BC Greek historian Herodotus to the Nasamonians of Cyrenaica), in which, on her wed-

A female ascetic depicted in a painting from Jaipur, Rajasthan, c.1760. Embracing virginity through asceticism is a choice made by devotees of many religions.

ding night, a woman lay with all her wedding guests before she was joined by her husband. Versions of this tradition have been reported in the 20th century (for example, among the Waitata and Waitavete of East Africa and the Aborigines of Australia), and most countries have attenuated forms of the custom, such as the practice of all the male guests kissing the bride at a European or North American wedding.

Sacred prostitutes

An ivory relief dating from c.800 BC, thought to depict the goddess Astarte, or Ishtar.

The earliest known term for priestess, in the language of ancient Sumer, may also be translated as "sacred prostitute". The goddess Inanna (forerunner of the Babylonian Ishtar), whom the Sumerian priestesses served, is herself referred to (in a hymn dating from 2300BC) as "the prostitute of the great god An". In one of the most famous documentations of sacred prostitution, the ancient Greek historian Herodotus (c.485–425 BC) describes how every Babylonian woman was compelled once in her lifetime to go to the temple of Ishtar and offer herself for a fee to any man who desired her. She could then place the fee on the altar as the price for her release. According to Herodotus, "tall, handsome women" soon managed to get home again, but others spent "as much as three or four years" in the temple before being able to buy their freedom.

There were also three classes of full-time "harlots" associated with the temple. The *ishtaritu* were virgins, servants of Ishtar, and reserved for the pleasure of the gods. The *qadishtu* were sacred prostitutes who were usually well born, well educated and land-owning, who would serve worshippers for a fee. The *harimtu* seem to have been semi-secular prostitutes who mostly worked out of the taverns, but could be called upon for special ceremonies or if demand grew too great at the temple. Sacred prostitution also flourished in ancient Egypt, especially associated with the god Ammon and the goddess Bast, and in ancient Greece. The temple of Aphrodite Porne at Corinth was said to contain 1,000 prostitutes at a time.

A temple prostitute was believed temporarily to embody the goddess she served while performing sex, and therefore to elevate the man who paid her into a divine state also. For this reason, sacred prostitution is generally considered to be a development of the sacred marriage: a mass-produced form of the archetypal fertility rite in which a king or priest and a priestess copulated, having assumed the roles of god and goddess (see pp.16–19). The participation of the king and a sacred prostitute was a vital part of the ancient Babylonian New Year ceremony of renewal (*akitu*). From at least the time of King Gudea (c.2100BC), sex with a sacred prostitute, personifying a goddess, was necessary for a monarch to legitimate his rule: otherwise, he would be worthless as a guarantor of fertility and prosperity.

Some groups in Borneo, such as the Olo Nyadju and the Kayan, have retained a tradition of initiating both priests and priestesses into prostitution. Mostly, however, the practice of sacred

A 17th-century brass plaque from Nigeria probably depicting the python god of Benin. The priestesses of the python god were held in high esteem as sacred prostitutes by the Ewe-speaking peoples of western Africa.

prostitution has died out; and it is dwindling in those parts of the world where it still retains a foothold.

A handful of 19th- and early 20th-century accounts indicate that forms of sacred prostitution existed until recently across much of western Africa. The Ewe-speaking peoples of southeast Ghana, Benin and Togo worshipped a python god, Dang-gbi, whose priestesses were also his wives. During their three-year training period, they were encouraged to prostitute themselves indiscriminately, but once accepted as priestesses were expected to sleep only with worshippers. Because these women had been driven to prostitution by a god, they were considered blameless, and were held in high esteem and deemed inviolable. The traditional gods of the Tshi-speaking groups of coastal Ghana were served by priests and priestesses. The priests could marry, but the priestesses were already married to the gods. They could, however, engage in sex with any man who attracted them. A report dating from as recently as the 1920s tells of the Ibo of Nigeria making a gift of 300 virgins to the shrine of their earth goddess. These women then had ritual sex with sterile men, who had come to them seeking a cure.

Male sacred prostitutes have not been recorded as frequently as females, although the eunuchs who lived in the temples of Cybele and Artemis (see p.16) were accused of acting as catamites (homosexual partners) for visitors to the temples. The Chaldean and Midianite cults that vied for popularity with early Judaism preferred male to female temple prostitutes, and in the parts of pre-conquest South and Meso-America

A bronze plaque of the Egyptian god Ammon, whose priestesses were often prostitutes, from the temple of Isis at Sakkara (c.760–656 BC).

where homosexuality was a part of public life (see pp. 46–7) male prostitutes took part in the sacred rites.

The temple prostitutes of India are called *devadasis*, or handmaids of god. They are the earthly counterparts of heavenly courtesans, or *apsaras*, who entertain Indra, master of the rains. These *apsaras* are themselves the personifications of rivers, and the sexual

A Greco-Roman theatrical half-mask made of fragments of coloured glass, from c.1st-century BC Egypt. Such masks would have been used by hetairai (courtesans).

activity of the *devadasis* symbolically brings on the life-giving rains. In Indian folklore, water is linked to sexuality, and opposed to heat, drought and asceticism. There are many tales of *devadasis* being sent to seduce an ascetic and

thereby "break the heat" of his asceticism, thought to be causing a drought.

Temple prostitution thrived in pre-colonial India, when a single temple might have had 400 *devadasis*. The institution eventually came under attack not only from outraged Europeans but from reform-minded Indians, and in 1947 the state of Madras passed the first anti-*devadasi* legislation (the Prevention of the Dedication of *Devadasis* Act), which made it a crime to dedicate *devadasis* to a temple. There are still *devadasis* in India, but even in those areas where temple prostitution is not against the

RITUAL DANCE

One of the *devadasi*'s ritual duties is to dance in the chamber outside the inner sanctum of the temple at the moment when food is offered

A Bharatha Natyam temple dancer from Tamil Nadu. Many different signs and gestures, made with the eyes as well as with the hands and fingers, are used to convey story and meaning in this type of dance.

to the god. The feeding of the god is the non-esoteric form of a secret Tantric rite, called the "five Ms" (see pp.150–55), and the dancing corresponds to the fifth part of this rite, *maithuna* (sexual congress).

Devadasis also used to dance for the king on ceremonial occasions, and dancing and prostitution were effectively synony-mous in India until the 1920s, when reformers made dance into an art that could

be performed even by high-caste women.

The *devadasis* call what they do simply *naca* (dance), but the Indian National Academy of Music and Dance identifies three classical styles based on the art of the *devadasi* (Odissi from Orissa, Bharatha Natyam from Tamil Nadu and Manipuri from Manipur), in addition to Kathakali from Kerala and Kathak from northern India (which probably owes its origins to a different school of prostitution, the houris of the Mughal court). When reformers began campaigning to add Odissi to this list in the 1950s, the *devadasis* of Orissa were pointedly excluded from the workshops, seminars and debates.

law, the tradition is dying out. When the management of the Jagannatha temple in Puri, northeastern India, passed from the king of the region to the state government in the mid-1950s, an official census listed thirty *devadasis*. By the late 1970s there were only nine, aged from thirty-five to seventy.

Devadasis are traditionally recruited as children, being either dedicated to the gods by their parents, or adopted by existing *devadasis*. However, grown women, especially widows, are known to dedicate themselves. *Devadasis* must come from the "water-giving" castes (*panisprusya*) – those who can give water to *brahmins* (the priestly high caste). Yet the *brahmins* are forbidden to take water from them, for as *devadasis* they are without caste: in spite of the pleasure they afford the gods and the fruitfulness of what they do, they are considered intrinsically impure. They are not allowed into the inner sanctum of the temple, even on occasions when that right is granted to lay visitors.

Devadasis are regarded as being married to the deity of the temple in which they serve, and as such they cannot marry a mortal man. They are supposed to have sex only with the earthly manifestations of the gods: the king and the *brahmin* priests, but this rule is rarely followed. Nevertheless, the comment by the 18th-century missionary Abbé Dubois, that "although originally they appear to have been intended for the gratification of the *brahmins* only, they are now obliged to extend their favours to all who solicit them", is merely

---

THE WHORE OF BABYLON

Judaism expressed the relationship between Jehovah (God) and his people, Israel, as a marriage. Those who strayed from the religion were spoken of as adulterers, gone whoring after other gods, as in the 8th century BC when the Canaanite fertility god Baal was adopted in place of Jehovah. The marriage of the prophet Hosea was made a symbol of the marriage between Jehovah and faithless Israel when the prophet was told: "Go, take thee a wife of whoredoms and children of whoredoms; for the land hath committed great whoredoms, departing from the Lord." The Judaic disapproval of prostitution also has a clear political basis, in that prostitutes were often the priestesses of rival cults, such as Canaanism, in which sexual rites played an important part.

Babylon itself, which held the Israelites in captivity from 586 to 539BC, was depicted in the Bible as a whore. Babylon the Whore, or the Whore of Babylon, later became identified with ancient Rome, embodying vice, corruption and evil, and eventually became a label for any state or organization considered corrupt. In the book of Revelation, Babylon is described as "the mother of whores and every obscenity", and its destruction is prophesied.

A Protestant vision of the Whore of Babylon riding the seven-headed beast, from the Luther Bible (c.1530). Wearing a papal crown, she is a metaphor for the Roman Catholic Church.

polemic. An officer of the king, called a *dosandi pariccha*, polices the sexual relationships of the *devadasis*, and punishes them if they have sex with men from an impure caste or with outsiders. "Concubine" would perhaps be a more appropriate term for the *devadasi* than "prostitute". She is supported by the temple and the king, and although her lovers often give her gifts, it is not a straightforward commercial exchange. In her role as the goddess, a *devadasi* might be worshipped by pilgrims without any sexual contact taking place. The pilgrim washes the *devadasi*'s feet, sips some of the water and takes the remainder home as sacred. Pilgrims make offerings of food to the *devadasi*, and eat whatever she leaves, known as *adharamruta*, "nectar from the lower lip".

RED-LIGHT DISTRICTS

The brothels of China, recognized by the red silk lanterns hanging outside their doors, may have comprised the first red-light districts. They were popular with husbands who were tired of the disciplines of Taoist sacred sex. Prostitutes, having been with many men, were thought to have so much female essence that they would more than compensate a man for male essence lost by careless ejaculation (see pp.138–43).

The Japanese geisha was a singer and dancer rather than a prostitute, offering entertainment as well as sex. Geisha houses were part of *Ukiyo* (floating world): the pleasant, if unstable, 17th-century urban society, with its tea-rooms, bath-houses and brothels (see below, *The Gay Quarters of Kyoto*, a 17th-century screen), where elaborate manners were elevated to serious ritual. Based on a pun between floating and sorrowful, *Ukiyo* came from the Buddhist "sorrowful world" of transience, dust and grief.

The Undivided Self

Male and female are commonly seen, in cultures worldwide, as the two complementary principles on which the universe is built. Every property, every phenomenon, can be attributed to one of them. For example, in a number of Asian Tantric philosophies, the sun and practicality (among other things) are male, while the moon and wisdom are female. The sex drive itself may consequently be portrayed as a kind of magnetic force, a will to unite these opposites to achieve a form of completeness, which, among the cultures that strive for it, is comparable to a state of divinity. At various times, among different peoples, ritualized sex has also been used to unite the individual human spirit with those of other humans; with the spirit that runs through the animal kingdom; with the spirit that courses through the earth; or with the spirits that are the gods themselves.

According to Hindu myth, Ayyappan was born from the union of Vishnu and Shiva: since both deities are male, one of them (Vishnu) assumed a female form in order to conceive. In almost all the major Indo-European faiths there are instances of gods being depicted as hermaphroditic or as the union of male and female – an aspect of the tendency to perceive the universe as made up of complementary pairs. This modern Indian print depicts the deity Hari-Hara, a combination of Vishnu (Hari, dark blue) and Shiva (Hara, recognizable by the tiger skin and crescent moon, symbols of Shiva), emphasizing the complementarity of Vishnu as Preserver and Shiva as Destroyer.

Creation myths

Creation myths, like most stories of the gods, tend to be modelled on human behaviour, and as such can provide a portrait of a society, and especially of the relationship between the sexes. The Greek myth in Hesiod's *Theogony* (Birth of the Gods, *c.*700BC) recounts a common pattern of conflict and mistrust between generations, which is itself only the symptom of an endless conflict between male and female. In this myth, Gaia (the earth) was born of Chaos, and coupled with her own self-generated

first-born, Uranos (the sky). He pushed all the children she bore him back inside her, until she encouraged one of them, Kronos, to castrate his father. In his turn, Kronos ate the children born to him by Rhea, until he was overcome by one of their sons, Zeus. For his part, Zeus swallowed his first wife, Metis, when she became pregnant, and produced their child Athene from his own head. The myth reflects a culture that was obsessed by man's authority over woman; by treachery, bastardy and the uncertainties of fatherhood; and consequently by the male control of female reproductive powers – a control that was generally depicted as the triumph of civilization over nature.

Political changes, and consequent shifts in the relative status of the sexes, may be traced through the evolution of creation stories. In ancient Mesopotamia, where women had similar rights to men's, the world was thought to have been created by the goddess Tiamat. By *c.*1700BC, when Babylon was the dominant city in the region and men had claimed greater sexual and economic rights, Tiamat had become a monster, the embodiment of chaos, which the Babylonian god Marduk had to conquer and dismember to make the world. Elsewhere, as in parts of the South Pacific, a (male) figure must dive to the bottom of the (female) sea to draw up the land: again expressing the attitude that man must impose a pattern on, and draw meaning from, woman's chaotic fecundity.

Following the example of human behaviour, creation myths often describe a world created by the copulation of the sky and the earth, the sun

AFRICAN TWINS

The creation story of the Dogon of Mali was kept secret from outsiders until the 1940s. In it, the god Amma made the earth from clay. The earth was female; her vagina was an anthill and her clitoris a termite mound. The lonely Amma wanted sex with the earth, but the termite mound blocked him and he cut it down. This clumsy union resulted in a single child: the deceitful jackal. The second conception occurred without mishap, and produced the Nummu, a pair of twins which was yet a perfect, androgynous unit.

When Amma created humans, the Nummu foresaw that twin births would be rare, but was worried in case single births produced more unbalanced creatures like the jackal. So the Nummu gave the first humans their souls by having them lie on a drawing of two figures copulating. In this way, humans were endowed with two souls, one of each sex, so that they should not be unbalanced even if born alone (see p.37).

A Dogon sculpture that is placed before a shrine, representing the power of the primordial twins.

In the book of Genesis, there are two accounts of the creation of the world. In the first, God created the world in stages over six days, pronouncing each stage good. He made the first human both male and female, and in his own image. The second account has earth and heaven made in a day, and contains the more familiar tale of the making of humanity: Adam, "of the earth", was moulded from dust and life was blown in through his nose. Eve, "life", was made from his rib, to be his "helper". This story is shown above, in a plate from the 9th-century Grandval Bible.

and the moon, or simply by a god and a goddess. The problem of where these creators themselves came from – of how something can come from nothing – is solved by supposing a complete, androgynous primordial being, which, because it contains all opposites, is in a sense also nothing. This being splits itself into male and female elements to begin the process of creation. The Egyptian Gnostic Valentinus wrote that Ennoia (Grace) was originally contained, with everything else, inside the Autopater (Father of All), until she "moved the Greatness to the desire to lie with her", and instigated the creation of the world. By extension, the original or primeval human is also widely depicted as hermaphroditic (see pp. 48–9). In the Hindu Brihadaranyaka Upanishad, the primal man, Purusha, takes no pleasure in solitude and divides into male and female. However, the female half has misgivings about the incestuous nature of their union (see pp. 120–23): "How can he embrace me having produced me from himself?" She hides by transforming herself into a series of animals, but he always finds her, changes into the male of the species and couples with her, thereby procreating the animal kingdom. Even the Jewish Yahweh (Jehovah), one of the most overtly masculine of father-gods, originally had a feminine side (see p.49).

In one Egyptian creation myth, the world is created by the copulation of the sky and the earth, Nut and Geb, as depicted in this Egyptian papyrus painting (c.1250BC). Unusually, in this myth, the sky is female and the earth male.

Does the spirit have a sex?

Spirit may be fire, or breath, or marrow, or semen, or all four simultaneously. It may be a ghost, animating the machine of the body, or a purified form of that body. It may be an illusion, or the product of illusion, or the only true reality.

The most common representation of the spirit is as light, and by extension, fire. A "perpetual fire" is a recurrent symbol of immortality, and ecstatic dancers, shamans and wonder-workers often demonstrate their control over spirits by manipulating fire. The Indo-European root-word for god, *diew*, means "the shining one", and the Indian Vedic god Agni is literally the sacrificial flame. One of Agni's names is Hiranyagarbhi, "golden germ": he is compared to lightning and to orgasm, and as the blazing sky-bull he spills his seed to fertilize the earth. The theme of impregnation by fire – or impregnation as a way of passing on soul-fire – is echoed in the phallic Shiva, carrying a flame in his hand. However, the idea is not restricted to India. The Greek philosopher Plato described giving birth as passing on a torch, and the Roman historian Pliny told how Servius Tullius, sixth king of Rome, was begotten by a phallus of fire. Among the Bantu and others, lighting a fire by rubbing sticks together is a ritual symbol of sexual intercourse.

In Vedic and ancient Greek sacrifices, fat, bones and marrow were offered to the gods, and the meat was kept for human consumption. This was not to short-

The Alaskan Inuit believed they each have several souls. This otter mask opens to reveal the spirit's human face.

change the gods but was because marrow and fat, which burned easily, were held to be a source of fire, and therefore spirit, making them an appropriate gift for spiritual beings. The identification of bones and fire is clear in the pre-Buddhist Japanese Saito Goma cult, in which ninety-one pieces of wood, standing for the bones of the body, were used to make a fire that symbolized the formation of a human in the womb.

In many cultures, bone marrow was confused with brain matter, and both were believed to be the source of semen (see pp.40–45). To the ancient Greeks, seed was soul, or psyche; it was stored in the head and passed on by the male. According to this belief, a sexual feature (that is, semen) was the very stuff of the soul, and women were held to possess smaller souls than men, or even no souls at all.

The idea of the "ghost in the machine" goes back at least as far as Mosaic times and the Hebrew belief in *ruah*, a procreative breath, residing in the body but with its own innate wisdom. St Paul made this idea more explicit. The body was compared to a tent or garment in which the soul resided. Paul ignored Christ's comment that the dead join God immediately, and reasserted an older idea that they lie "asleep", awaiting a mass resurrection into new, "spiritual bodies". The nature of these spiritual bodies exercised theologians for centuries. Irenaeus of Lyons (*c.*AD

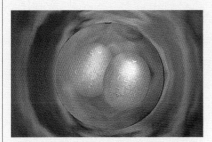

A human embryo at the two-cell stage. Its sex is already determined; there is no general agreement as to when, if ever, the foetus gains a soul.

140–200) imagined them as fleshly, immortal, healthy, sexual, fertile and capable of sensory pleasures (resembling the souls in the Muslim paradise; see pp.76–7). St Augustine, 200 years later, declared that "celestial bodies" precluded "celestial flesh": heaven was populated with sexless, immaterial souls, taking pleasure in contemplating God. The Chinese – among many others, such as the Yuit of Alaska and the voodoo worshippers of Haiti (see p.59) – have more than one ghost in their machine, and, typically, one of these will possess an individual's characteristics, including their sex.

None of these beliefs provides a convincing explanation of how the spirit interacts with the body. Modern Western philosophy of mind suggests that the sense of soul, spirit, mind or ego is a kind of illusion – the by-product of a hugely complicated system (the brain and the senses) whose parts constantly interrogate each other and record the results. It is the continuity of these

records that constitutes an awareness of self, or "spirit". It is impossible to determine whether this "spirit" has a sex: some sexual drives and preferences seem to be innate, depending on the mechanical workings of the brain, while other sexual behaviour is apparently the result of social (that is, external) forces.

Classical Buddhism also denies any substantial reality to the ego, and has an intriguingly similar, causal account of the illusory origins of the soul. Ignorance gives rise to certain *karma*-structures (patterns of action): it is these that generate consciousness, which gives rise to name-and-form (physical and mental phenomena), which creates feelings and cravings. If these can be suppressed, the process can be reversed, and the soul can ultimately return to non-being.

A 19th-century Tibetan thanka *(cloth painting) depicting Padmasambhava dwelling in his Pure Land Paradise. In Pure Land Buddhism, souls are believed to have an independent existence.*

Marks of initiation

Ritual acts express important social ideas symbolically, by mapping them onto the physical world (including the human body). Because every society has its own specific notion of the relationship – or antagonism – between the human spirit and the human body, concepts of spirituality that legitimate the social and moral order of a people are often written in the flesh. In this way, rituals link the social and the biological, so that the former comes to seem as inevitable as the latter.

The initiations that mark an individual's movement from one social/biological state to another – such as the transition from child to adult – usually have three definite stages. First, the initiate's departure from his or her previous state of being – a symbolic "death" – is signalled by washing, head-shaving, circumcision or other forms of marking. In the second stage a liminal, or boundary, state is entered – a period of fear and confusion: the initiate may be blindfolded and led into the wilderness. Finally, rebirth into the new state may involve being anointed, eating special foods or wearing new clothes.

The circumcision of boys, the rite in which the foreskin is cut away, can occur at various ages: for example, it is performed on babies in Judaism and on pre-pubescents in Madagascar. Most typically, it is a component of puberty rites, notably in Africa and Australasia, in which fortitude in the face of the pain caused by the procedure is seen as a necessary part of manhood. It may be mirrored, especially in parts of Africa,

Boys in North Sotho, South Africa, awaiting their mass circumcision, a ritual that will usher them from boyhood to manhood.

by the "circumcision" of girls. The Pokot of Kenya initiate a girl by excising her labia in public, during which she is not supposed to move or cry out, and shames her family if she does. So-called female circumcision has varying degrees of severity. It may involve the cutting away of the clitoris (clitoridectomy), or of the minor labia, or both. Infibulation is frequently performed, in which the vagina is sewn closed after the operation, or bound so as to heal with a scar that will bleed the next time the woman has intercourse. Among many peoples, including the Pokot, this is considered a way of recovering the woman's virginity. Pokot women usually marry while still bearing the scars of their initiations.

Both male circumcision and clitoridectomy are ways of emphasizing

Australian Arunta men prepare for an initiation ritual by painting marks on their bodies that relate to their mythological ancestors.

and defining adult masculinity and femininity, in that they remove those parts of the genitalia that most resemble the genitalia of the other sex. The Dogon of Mali believe that each boy or girl is born with two souls (see p.32): a boy has a female soul in his foreskin, and a girl has a male soul in her clitoris, but humans are not capable of maintaining this double nature into adulthood, and so the contrary souls have to be cut away. The Ndembu of Zambia maintain that the circumcised penis more closely resembles the erect penis, and is thus more potent.

Australian Arunta adolescents are taken for their circumcision by men who swing cut sticks called bull-roarers, producing a noise believed to simulate the fearsome voices of the spirits. The boys believe that it is the spirits that

SPIRITUAL POTENCY

Sexual elements are a common feature of maturity rites, but are not restricted to them. For the Mandan Native North Americans, sexual intercourse was a way of transferring power. Mandan society was stratified into societies or fellowships, and a man who desired power might sleep with the wife of a warrior who belonged to a higher-ranking society than his own. Alternatively, he could "purchase" his way

into a higher-ranking society by offering his wife to a man in that society. This was not considered a straightforward exchange of sexual favours for preferment: rather, the higher-ranking man would pass on some of his power to the woman, who transferred it to her husband when they next had intercourse.

Initiation into the secret Mau Mau society of Kenya includes mimicking intercourse by pushing a reed into a goat's hollow backbone, called the *ngata*, which

represents a sacred stone. Here, the symbolic sexual act is performed to quicken magical powers that will bind the oaths of loyalty which are to be made.

Initiates into spirit-possession cults, such as that of the Nyoro of Uganda, may see themselves as married to a particular spirit (see p.57). Part of a Nyoro woman's initiation involved a senior male medium placing a temporary curse on her, which he later lifted by sleeping with her.

perform the operation. However, for Arunta boys, circumcision is only the first part of their maturity ritual. A few weeks later, they are again taken away by the men, and their penises are subincised: the whole of the urethra is slit from below with a stone knife. The blood is collected, and referred to as menstrual blood, and the wound is a "penis womb" or a "penis vagina". For the Arunta, a boy's maturity does not just involve becoming a man, but becoming a being that contains both male and female. This symbolic hermaphroditism can be found in more partial and less drastic forms in other parts of the world. In some Xingu groups of the Amazon, a boy's ears are pierced as part of his initiation, and the blood is equated with menstruation.

The Arunta subincision may be a specific response to the castration anxiety induced by the sight of a bleeding vagina (see pp.124–5). Subincised Arunta men have said, "We are not afraid of the bleeding vagina, we have it ourselves. It does not threaten the

A 5th-century BC statue of the Phrygian earth goddess Cybele, whose male followers would castrate themselves as part of an orgiastic initiation into her cult.

penis: it is the penis." (However, some Arunta claim instead that they are trying to imitate the penis – and gain the sexual prowess – of the kangaroo.) Sigmund Freud believed that castration anxiety was a universal masculine trait, related to the Oedipal phase of development (see pp.106–7), and that circumcision among the Australian Aborigines was a symbolic act of castration, making use of such anxiety to maintain social order. The psychologist Bruno Bettelheim (1903–90) disputed this interpretation, pointing out how eager the young men were to undergo initiation. But there have been cases where initiates have welcomed even castration, or have castrated themselves during orgiastic frenzy.

Followers of the ancient Phrygian mother goddess Cybele were known as Galli, or Corybantes. In one legend, Cybele drove her unfaithful lover Attis into a fury so that he emasculated himself, and he was on the point of suicide when Cybele changed him into a tree. Castration became an aspect of the initiation rites into the cult of Cybele. At the wild and frenetic Corybantic ceremonies, young men who had only come as spectators would be driven to such a pitch of excitement that they would rush out of the crowd and seize a cere-

Initiations, such as this one in Sierra Leone, often allow women temporary social licence.

A young Apache girl on the fourth and last day of her puberty ceremony. Her face is smeared with mud, indicating the entry into her of the earth mother or goddess.

RITUAL SEGREGATION

Some peoples, such as the North American Hopi, initiate boys and girls into adulthood together. However, the majority of initiation rites are for only one of the sexes, and even if males and females are to be initiated at the same time, they are usually rigidly segregated, and are allowed no polluting contact with each other. The Gisu of Kenya consider the neighbouring Sebei barbarous for initiating girls. The Sebei describe the Gisu as the barbarians, because to them it is obvious that males and females must both be ritually introduced to their adult sexual roles; but the Sebei nevertheless keep the rites for each sex secret from the other.

Because girls and women undergo far more clearly defined physical changes than boys and men – such as the onset of menstruation, pregnancy and childbirth – their initiations are often individual, domestic affairs, undertaken when the biological time is right. It is much more usual for boys to experience socially prescribed group initiations, in which the members might show a wide range of physical maturity. Even where girls do undergo group initiation, as in the African Bemba, there is an emphasis on the transfer of domestic wisdom.

monial sword. Such an event was described by the 2nd-century AD Greek writer Lucian: "He takes it and castrates himself and runs wild through the city bearing in his hands what he has cut off. He casts it into any house at will, and from this house he receives women's raiment and ornament." Initiated male Corybantes all wore women's clothing (a practice not uncommon in orgiastic rituals; see pp.54–9). Even those men who visited the temple of Cybele but did not make the supreme commitment were expected to perform the symbolic castration of shaving off their hair (an act that

evolved into the symbolic castration of the monk's tonsure).

The practice of self-castration has been interpreted as a sacrifice of the seed vessels to the deity, but it has also been seen as a particularly extreme way of avoiding defilement through sex, and as a positive way of conserving seed, or "soul-stuff" (see pp.40–45). The Greeks thought that the testes did not produce semen, but were a temporary reservoir, whose removal prevented issue but allowed the manufacture of semen to continue; they believed that the tendency of eunuchs to grow fat was due to the accumulation of unspent seed.

The divine seed

The Birth of Venus (c.1485), by Sandro Botticelli. According to classical legend, when Kronos, father of Zeus, castrated his own father Uranos (see p.62), he cast the severed genitals into the sea. They floated on the water, generating a foam from which, unmothered, Aphrodite (Venus) emerged.

One of the earliest and most persistent sexual myths is that semen is the fundamental stuff of life: not only in the sense that it is necessary for conception, but also because it resembles the matter of the brain, and therefore is the substance of the soul. There may have been an even more ancient belief, the relics of which may still exist: that semen plays no part in the creation of life at all.

In 1903, the anthropologist W.E. Roth claimed that the Aborigines of Tully River in Australia were ignorant of the connection between copulation and pregnancy. The women of Tully River believed that they became pregnant because they sat over a fire while cooking a fish that had been given to them by the child's prospective father, or because they went out hunting for frogs,

or because they had a dream about the child being put inside them. The actual, as opposed to the social, father of the child was the spirit known as the Rainbow Serpent. Some years later, the anthropologist Bronislaw Malinowski (1884–1942) reported similar beliefs among the Trobrianders of Papua New Guinea, whom he studied between 1915 and 1918. There, the child was believed to originate with a spirit ancestor of the mother, and although the mother's vagina had to be opened so that the child-spirit might enter her, the use of a man's penis was not strictly necessary: the woman could perform the act herself with the aid of inanimate objects.

These findings were attacked by subsequent investigators, as springing from the arrogance of cultural evolutionists who wanted to portray traditional peoples as corresponding to particular (in this case matriarchal) stages in the development of Western society. The earlier researchers were also criticized as naive for thinking that their informants believed literally in what they said, independently of the social, ritual and storytelling contexts in which their comments were made. Subsequent investigation showed that various Aborigines had, parallel to their religious beliefs, a notion of biological conception. The cultural evolutionists asserted that this was a muddled version of what had been learned from missionaries. As recently as 1975, it was claimed that the Bellonese of the Solomon Islands were ignorant of the role of sex in conception before they were taught by Christian missionaries. One reason for this ignorance, it was stated, was the absence on their island of large mammals and livestock which could be observed in order to discover the biological facts. Those who believe that neolithic hunting communities were matriarchies based on the perceived power of the woman to create life unaided also consider that patriarchy developed with the first herders, who learned about the male role in conception from watching their flocks.

These speculations may seem fanciful, but in the face of a compelling system of belief, knowledge that springs from evidence is often disregarded, forgotten or explained away. It may be that this was the case with Malinowski and the other cultural evolutionists, who interpreted evidence in such a way as to

HEADHUNTERS

The identification of brain, bone marrow and semen as the same, indivisible stuff of life, or soul-matter, may stretch back more than 250,000 years, to the Neanderthals who, fossil evidence suggests, engaged in ritual brain-eating. In a manner common to hunting cultures (see pp.12–15), in which the killing of an animal is considered to involve a transfer of power from prey to hunter, the Celts seem to have associated taking a man's head with gaining the potency of his spirit, thus increasing the headhunter's own fertility.

This is also the motivation for much of the headhunting activity that survived well into the 20th century, from mainland Southeast Asia and Indonesia to New Guinea and Melanesia (there are still reports of the practice in isolated areas). The Dyaks of Borneo and the Alfurs of Minahassa considered it necessary for a man to take a head before he could marry. The Dyaks also thought that a newly taken head made their women fertile, the rice grow and the woods teem with animals. The Asmat of New Guinea, who were headhunters until the 1950s, used to place the decorated head of a victim between the thighs of an adolescent boy to initiate him into manhood. His genitals absorbed the vitality of the head at the same time that the ritual gave him the name of its original owner.

Elders of the Ymendi people of New Guinea preparing feathers for a ritual headdress.

produce the results they expected: but it could equally be the case with the peoples they investigated. For example, in the Trobriand Islands, divorce petitions brought by husbands returning from long periods overseas and finding their wives pregnant can still be thrown out of court if a wife's mother testifies that the pregnancy is magical. Research into the Trobrianders from the late 1980s suggests a subtle differentiation between conception and pregnancy. They say that a spirit makes a woman conceive, but that semen nourishes and shapes the foetus during frequent post-conception intercourse.

Historically, the most common attitude to be recorded is the exact opposite of this. According to the ancient Greek writer Diodorus, the Egyptians believed that the father alone was the "author of generation" (an attitude mirrored in the myth of Atum; see p.127), and the mother merely provided a nest and nourishment for the foetus. Aristotle (384–322BC) taught that the psyche (or soul) was contained in the seed as it passed from a man's head, via his bone marrow and his testicles (which were merely a semen reservoir). This is one reason why Christians were instructed by the Church not to spill their seed wantonly. Another reason is that, as the stuff of the brain, semen is finite and irreplaceable (see pp.126–7). Although this was the prevalent view in Christian Europe, it occasionally went out of fashion, and the 13th-century theologian Duns Scotus expressed a commonplace of his time when he

The Greek god Mercury with innumerable phalluses growing out of his head (above), and a panel from the Gundestrup Cauldron (left), a 4th- or 3rd-century BC Danish cult vessel, possibly depicting the Celtic god Cernunnos. The antlers of Cernunnos are phallic symbols and images of fertility: like Mercury's phalluses, they are generated from his head, because of its concentration of brain–marrow–semen matter.

wrote that too much continence could be harmful, because semen that was hoarded too long became poisonous. Beliefs about the irreplaceability of seed resurfaced during the Renaissance, and can still be encountered in some modern Western communities.

Similar attitudes exist today among numerous peoples of New Guinea, whose men blame women for killing them slowly through sex. They accept that this is necessary, however, as the women convert the semen they take into milk for the next generation. These same peoples believe that adolescent boys have to be inseminated in order to become men (see pp.46–7). Among some New Guineans, such as the Keraki, this ritual insemination is believed to carry the risk that the boy will become pregnant, and a lime-eating ceremony is performed to avert this possibility. Male pregnancy is also considered possible among a number of African peoples, such as the Ila of Zambia, who, as a consequence, outlaw homosexuality. Some of the Navajo used to state that a man would risk becoming pregnant if he copulated with the woman on top, or allowed a menstruating woman to step over him as he lay on the ground.

The Taoists and the Hindus believe that semen is a rare, precious substance, which should not be wasted (see pp.138–43), but they maintain that it is possible to regenerate it, and improve its quality. A Taoist who wishes to

RUSSIAN DOLLS

In 1675, the Dutch microscopist Antony van Leeuwenhoeck discovered spermatozoa (or as he called them, "animalcules") swimming in a drop of seminal fluid. Three years earlier, Regnier de Graaf had discovered the ovum and that it travels from the ovary to the womb, lured, he thought, by the scent of semen, or *aura seminalis*. There followed nearly a century of argument between ovists, who thought the egg contained a tiny complete human being, just waiting to grow, and spermists, who placed this homunculus in the head of the sperm. The philosopher Gottfried Leibniz (1646–1716) pointed out that if either the sperm or the egg contained a tiny human being, complete with its soul, then that tiny human had to contain another tiny human, like a nest of Russian dolls, and on to infinity. The fusion of the egg and the sperm – proof of the involvement of both sexes – was observed in 1854.

An alchemical plate dating from 1628. Some alchemists and sorcerers claimed to be able to grow homunculi from inanimate matter.

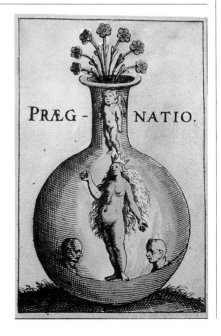

impregnate his wife should first have sex with a number of different women, without ejaculating. In this way their yin, or female energy, thickens his semen and makes it more potent. According to one Hindu *brahmin* (the priestly high caste), it takes forty drops of blood, coagulating and purifying in the body for forty days, to make a single drop of semen. Unused semen returns to, and nourishes, the head.

Throughout the native communities of North and South America there are comparable notions about power residing in the seed, with some interesting local variations. The Bellacoola of the northwest coast of North America practised a procedure known as *sxetsta*, or ceremonial chastity, in which abstinence was punctuated at ceremonially appropriate moments by ritual intercourse (*xoldujat*), which was believed to amplify enormously the power that had been built up while retaining the semen. The most comprehensive mythology concerning semen is found among the Kágaba of Colombia. They believe that humans have copulated over every part of the earth's surface, and that semen has soaked into the ground until it is

RIGHT An anatomical drawing (c.1492–94) of sexual intercourse from one of Leonardo da Vinci's notebooks. Despite performing many dissections, and notwithstanding his remarkable powers of observation, Leonardo depicts spinal ducts to the penis that do not actually exist. He did this because, influenced by ancient Greek authorities such as Galen and Hippocrates, he believed there were "two causes" of existence, one infused from the testes and the other – the carrier of the soul – infused from the spinal cord.

now completely saturated. For any more semen to enter the earth would cause it to break open, at the very least releasing sickness and plague, and possibly destroying the world and everything in it. As a result, masturbation is a terrible sin; and, during sex, special magic stones have to be placed beneath the genitals to catch any spillage. In order to expiate their sexual sins, the Kágaba have to make an offering of semen to Heiséi, their spirit master of sexuality and sexual aberrations. However, the semen that is offered to Heiséi has to be collected during the performance of the same sinful act for which atonement is being made: thus, among the Kágaba, the only way that a sin can be expiated is by repeating it precisely.

WOMEN WITH TESTICLES

Because semen is the universal soul-matter, it follows that women as well as men possess it (although some contemporaries of Aristotle took the opposite position, asserting that women had no souls). Among the Turkana of northern Kenya it is thought

that both the sexes have enough semen in their bodies – in their brains and the marrow of their bones – to keep them alive, but that only men have enough excess semen to impregnate a woman, whereas a woman's own surplus brain-matter becomes her menstrual blood.

When the early Christian Alexandrians discovered the ovaries, they described them

as poor copies of the testes, holding small amounts of watery semen which was neither as virtuous nor as vigorous as that of the male. Later, a 16th-century Spanish anatomical manual described the ovaries grudgingly, expressing the hope that "women might not become all the more arrogant for knowing that they also, like men, have testicles".

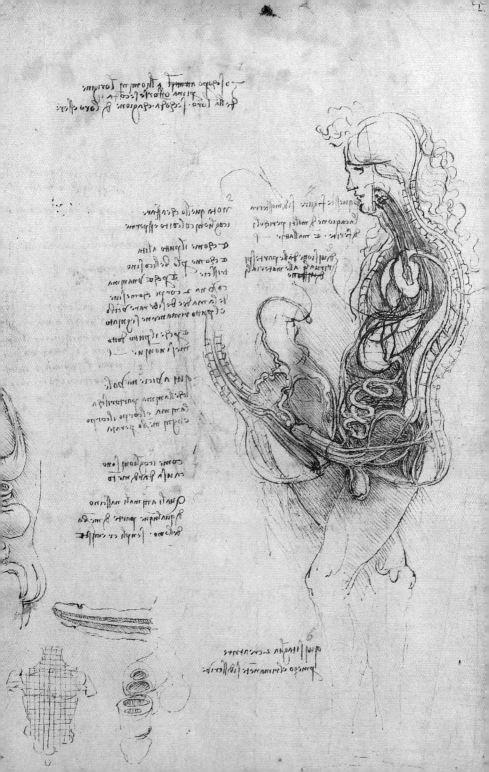

Homosexuality

Homosexuality has existed at all times and in all cultures, generally ignored or repressed, but occasionally institutionalized, particularly between males.

Because of laws that fined or imposed marriage on men caught having sex with single women, wealthy Mayan families in the 15th century provided their adolescent sons with male slaves to attend to their sexual needs until a marriage was arranged. For the classical Greeks, homosexuality was a more exalted affair, although the Athenians disapproved of sodomy, and believed that the submissive partner removed himself from the status of a male citizen and joined the lower ranks of women and foreigners.

The only sexual relation that was considered to be between social equals was pederasty, between an adult male (the *erastes*, lover) and a youth (the *eromenos*, beloved), whose "moral perfection" was to be cultivated by the lover. This was the only relationship that was usually consummated face to face (interfemorally, with the penis of one clasped between the thighs of the other), and its central quality was one of mutual dignity. The beloved did not yield to the will of the lover, and although he could feel affection for the older man, was not supposed to share in his desire.

Plato, in his conception of homosexual love as the fuel that drives the soul toward knowledge (see p.103),

This Greek cup dating from c.480BC depicts interfemoral sex, with the beloved staring at his lover dispassionately. In his Symposium, Xenophon says, "The boy does not share in the man's pleasure in intercourse, as a woman does; cold sober, he looks upon the other drunk with sexual desire." The lover was older and wiser than the beloved, but his slavery to his own desire preserved the notional equality between them that was so important to the Greeks.

devised a theoretical relationship in which both parties were simultaneously lover and beloved. However, their masculinity and dignity could only be preserved by leaving their desire unconsummated. The physical body, said Plato, must remain the slave of reason, and mutual desire between men should be used only to liberate both their souls.

For the Sambia of New Guinea, semen itself is soul-matter (see pp.40–45) – a magical substance that transforms but is not

A double-chambered ceramic vessel depicting an act of homosexual fellatio, from 14th-century Peru. This may have had fertility connotations, associating the liquor it contained with sperm.

depleted by the body in which it circulates; yet neither can it be created. Therefore, from their first stage of initiation between the ages of seven and ten, boys perform regular fellatio on adolescent youths and older men, in order to become inseminated so that they might mature and become men themselves. They also acquire ancestral spirit familiars in the seed. An older man who tries to receive semen from a younger man is regarded as a monster. Among other New Guinea tribes, such as the Keraki of the Trans-Fly River Delta, the insemination of boys is accomplished through sodomy. Ritual acts of masculinization such as these must be kept secret from women and children, on pain of death.

In such examples of institutional, age-based homosexuality, where an older man undertakes the initiation of a boy into manhood, neither participant adopts the role of a female. Gender-based ritual homosexuality does exist, however, as exemplified by the North American berdache (see pp.48–53), and by some Melanesian peoples, such as those of the New Hebrides.

Female homosexuality has been less institutionalized, although a few Melanesian peoples may practise it as part of

An Indian album painting dating from c.1850. Lesbian scenes were a relatively common subject of Indian eroticism. Often a couple would be shown being watched by the god Krishna.

girls' initiation ceremonies. The Athenians thought lesbianism was especially common in Sparta, where, according to Plutarch "even respectable women became infatuated with girls". It did not seem to occur to the disapproving Athenians that this behaviour could be the counterpart of their own pederasty.

The Greek poet Sappho is said to have run an academy for girls on the island of Lesbos in the 7th century BC. Her highly sensual poems deal with love, passion and jealousy; some scholars maintain that they are purely spiritual, but the Roman writer Apuleius thought them wanton and Ovid described them as a comprehensive guide to female homosexuality.

A HOMOSEXUAL GENE?

The possible existence of a gene causing homosexuality was suggested by Dr Dean Hamer in 1993. Through the passing on of genes, sex and reproduction were presented as ineluctable agents of fate. In fact, even the relatively mechanical immune system is controlled by hundreds of different genes, which themselves display polymorphism, or great variety. It is unlikely that any single gene accounts for more than a few per cent of any personality trait.

Hermaphroditism and transvestism

Androgyne, hermaphrodite and bisexual are interchangeable terms when applied to gods or other spiritual beings, each implying the fusion and encapsulation of both male and female characteristics. But human biological hermaphrodites are widely persecuted or killed in traditional societies, and surgically "corrected" in the West. At the same time, androgynous behaviour is often tolerated and even encouraged, in some societies, as being representative of spiritual hermaphroditism and spiritual completeness. Human bisexuals are simply those who desire both men and women.

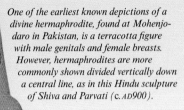

One of the earliest known depictions of a divine hermaphrodite, found at Mohenjo-daro in Pakistan, is a terracotta figure with male genitals and female breasts. However, hermaphrodites are more commonly shown divided vertically down a central line, as in this Hindu sculpture of Shiva and Parvati (c. AD900).

For the Greek philosopher Plato (*c*.429–*c*.347BC), the existence of a primeval hermaphroditic figure explained the often troublesome existence of love and attraction between the sexes. In his *Symposium*, he has the playwright Aristophanes tell the story of how once there were three kinds of being – male, female and hermaphrodite – each having four legs and four arms. They became too powerful, so Zeus split them in two. The parts derived from the whole men became pederasts, the parts from the whole women became lesbians and the parts from the hermaphrodites "who are nowadays regarded with scorn, gave rise to men who are woman-lovers and adulterers, and to women who are man-lovers and adulteresses". All sexual attraction is the desire of incomplete humans to fuse back into the original, eight-limbed state.

The idea of the hermaphroditic creator, whether as god or primal human (see pp.32–3), is widespread but not universal. It first appeared in ancient Mesopotamia, and the 20th-century German scholar Hermann Baumann claimed that it is restricted to those areas that, however indirectly, have been influenced by the so-called "high civilizations" of Central America, Southeast Asia and the Near East. Nevertheless, myths about such a figure are found throughout the ancient Indo-European world, as well as in North and South America, Africa, Australia and the Pacific Islands.

In Western Europe and the Near East, the idea of an androgynous god has largely been suppressed, but can still be traced

A linga *(phallus) within a* yoni *(vulva) symbolizing the universal union of male and female elements.*

through the writings of Jewish and Christian mystics. The early Mesopotamian accounts of the hermaphrodite creator are echoed in the Hebrew myth of Genesis, and the oldest existing commentaries state explicitly that God created the first man as androgynous, so that Adam "gave birth" to Eve. Further, since God created man in his image, the creator himself must have been androgynous. Jakob Boehme (1575–1624), was one of the more influential of many mystics who claimed that Christ was androgynous like his father, with male and female meeting in his soul. He wrote: "When Christ on the cross once more redeemed man's virgin male–female image, and coloured it with heavenly blood … Christ changed the sleeping Adam from being man and woman, back to his original angelic image." Boehme also propounded a form of Gnostic doctrine: that the virgin Wisdom (Sophia) was part of the primal man, but split from him when he tried to dominate her. His philosophy had a

SERPENTS OF AUSTRALIA

The serpent that created humanity in Aboriginal mythology is a masculine figure in southern parts of Australia. It is only on the northern margin of the continent that the serpent is a mother, or sometimes a bisexual being, revealing the influence of Indonesian and New Guinean voyagers who may have colonized this part of Australia until as recently as the 16th century.

major influence on 18th- and 19th-century theosophists, and on the Romantic movement, many of whose writers and thinkers believed that man would one day evolve into an androgynous state.

However, the Romantic ideal of androgyny had no impact on the cruel way in which living androgynes were treated, as demonstrated by the history of persecution recorded in the diaries of the 19th-century hermaphrodite, Herculine Barbin. Indeed, hermaphroditism has only been considered desirable as a purely spiritual state, and even then has often invoked a degree of fear.

Hermaphroditus was the child of the gods Hermes and Aphrodite, and possessed both male and female sexual organs. In this mural from the House of the Dioscuri, Pompeii, even the orgiastic god Pan is horrified by such a form. But there is evidence that, in the Hellenistic and Roman periods, Hermaphroditus was considered an erotic figure.

Societies that otherwise revere androgyny may put to death a baby that is born physically hermaphrodite, considering it a monster. It seems that the physical signs of a spiritual hermaphroditism cannot be natural, or innate: they must be part of a culturally mediated androgyny defined by dress and behaviour; and they should not be adopted voluntarily by the androgyne, but only at the instigation of society or the spirits.

In North America and Siberia, the shamans are overwhelmingly male, but some of them may wear women's clothes – or simulate menstruation or childbirth – during their rituals. These regions also contain permanently transvestite shamans, such as the "soft man" of the Siberian Chukchi. Youths who are to become soft men will be instructed to change sex by a *ke'let*, or spirit familiar, at the same time as their shamanic vocation manifests itself. This is considered a terrible fate, and Chukchi youths may choose to commit suicide before submitting to it.

There are several degrees of transvestite transformation for a soft man. The first simply involves the shaman braiding his hair like a woman. In the second, the shaman takes to wearing women's clothes. In the most complete transformation, he throws away his hunting paraphernalia and learns women's skills.

ANGELS AND ALIENS

The Christian *angelos* is a translation of the Hebrew word for messenger, *mal'ak*, and is a masculine noun. The messengers of God in the Bible have men's names, such as Gabriel, Raphael and Michael, but unclear or confusing forms. Sometimes their appearance was inappropriate for a religion that had embraced the Devil as its image of evil: Ezekiel describes the beings at the throne of God as having four faces, four wings and hooves – much like the Devil. So early Christian iconographers borrowed an existing inspirational winged figure as

The Three Archangels and Tobias *by Francesco Botticini (c.1446–97). The angels are highly feminized figures.*

the model for their angels: the pagan goddess Nike, or Victory. As a result, angels became depicted as feminized, sexually ambiguous figures. They were also desexed philosophically in the writings of early theologians, who contended that, unlike the souls of the virtuous reborn, they were unable even to kiss.

The androgyny of angels may possibly have influenced the steadily increasing number of reports of other messengers from outer space. Aliens, supposedly from other planets, are overwhelmingly described by those who claim to have met them as asexual beings with no visible genitals and large eyes.

His body changes and he loses his strength and becomes bashful and soft-spoken. At the same time, he begins to court young men – with great success because he is aided by his supernatural or *ke'le*-husband. After a time the soft man chooses a material husband. One Chukchi soft man, called E'chuk, claimed to have borne sons from his own body, but these were fathered by his *ke'le*-husband rather than by his material husband. Another soft man, called

A berdache of the Zuni people, named We-wa, to the left of the photograph, with a school group gathered around him.

Kee'ulin, married a woman who bore him several sons before he entered a marriage with another man, which lasted twenty years. Despite their bashfulness, which prevents them from engaging in normal shamanic rivalries, soft men are feared by untransformed shamans because they are so jealously protected by their spirit spouses.

The berdache, encountered throughout North America under a variety of names, and fulfilling a variety of roles, is usually a transvestite male, although some dress as men or women according to whim, and others as old men. Lakota *winktes*, Navajo *nadles* and Cheyenne *he man ehs* have ritual functions; the Crow *badé* plays no part in ceremonials but is socially respected. Apaches and Pinas seem to be the only Native Americans to have actively despised the berdache. There is also a berdache tradition among the Aleuts and other Alaskans. Female transvestites have been represented among traditional North Amer-

ican groups, but they adopted ritual functions only in rare cases – such as the Kutenai warrior known as Manlike Woman, who started a Messianic cult among the Mackenzie River Athabascans in 1812.

Berdaches have survived in some Native American groups into the present day, and their numbers have probably increased with the modern growth of interest in shamanism, and because they have been reclaimed as a positive symbol by Native American – and other – gays. The tradition died out some time ago in much of the far north, although the berdache retains an enduring role in folklore. In the early part of the 20th century, transvestite men were regarded as the most powerful shamans on St Lawrence Island (part of the Chukchi culture area of the Bering Strait), despite homosexuality in general being frowned on. There are also legends of ritual homosexuality and transvestism among eastern and central Inuit.

Berdaches were held in high esteem among most Native American groups. They were considered powerful medicine, and were taken on war parties and hunting trips, although they were not expected to participate. They were believed to be skilled doctors and experts at love magic, and to perform women's work so well that a typical Plains compliment to a skilful wife would be that "she does beadwork as fine as a berdache". Among some groups, such as the Navajo, a berdache in the family was taken as a guarantee of wealth. The berdache was considered such an asset to the community that a number of groups, such as the Lakota and the Omaha (and, in the far north, the Koniag), made it compulsory for any young man who had a certain

kind of dream to become one. A typical story was that, like all boys at puberty, the berdache-to-be had gone on a quest to experience a vision and gain his manhood. The moon appeared to him and offered him a hunter's bow, but as he reached to take it the moon crossed her hands and gave him instead an elk-rib scraping knife or some other woman's tool.

Berdaches could marry, and in the case of the Navajo, who practised serial monogamy, could marry a number of men. These marriages attracted a great deal of comment, but it was always the husband who was mocked, never the berdache. The husband consoled himself that the mockery was fuelled by envy because the berdache was considered to be such a desirable wife.

HIJRAS

Male transvestites, known as *hijras*, are found throughout India and in neighbouring countries. Most of them make their living as prostitutes, and although in modern India they are widely stigmatized, they are still regularly called upon to perform their ancient ritual function of singing and dancing in a house where a male child has been born. Like temple prostitutes (see pp.24–9), although they are impure, *hijras* are considered auspicious, and are thought to bring fertility, health and prosperity to the child.

Many *hijras* claim that they were born with deformed genitals, and that this is how they found their calling. In general, however, it is the

caste duty of a *hijra* to perform an act of self-castration, while sitting before a picture of the goddess Bahachura Mata and repeating her name, so as to identify with her. The *hijra*'s

Hijras *in Bangladesh. Many still consider it lucky to have a* hijra *attend a wedding ceremony.*

reproductive capacity is thought of as having been sacrificed to the goddess, and so, although the *hijra* is sterile, he is regarded as a source of general fecundity. (This is, again, similar to the temple prostitute, who brings the rains but, if she wants children, is supposed to adopt rather than procreate.)

Similar ritual transvestites can also be found in traditional communities in Korea, Vietnam, Celebes and Kalimantan. Among some African peoples, such as the Zulu, fortune-telling can be performed only by transvestites.

GENDER AND PERFORMANCE

A ritual transvestite, such as the berdache, is usually represented as a melding of the two complementary categories of male and female. However, the transvestite may represent a "third sex" or a "third term", not in the sense of being a blurring of male and female, but in the sense of standing outside – and casting doubt on – this entire two-fold system of classification. The Crow word for berdache, *badé*, means "not man, not woman", and the Cree word *ayekkwew* can mean either "man and woman" or "neither man nor woman". The Navajo *nadle* ("transformed person") can change (sexual) persona, much like an actor, by changing costume. The *nadle* is addressed by male or female terms depending on whether he/she is wearing men's or women's clothes.

Some commentators have suggested that transvestism in general is an attack on the

A poster dating from 1896 by Alfons Mucha depicting the actress Sarah Bernhardt dressed to play the male lead-role in the play Lorenzaccio.

widely held idea that human behaviour has to be classified as male or female, or even a combination of the two. In the words of one cultural critic, cross-dressing suggests that "gender exists only in representation – or performance". As such, it is also an attack on the whole concept of a stable personal identity: it questions the possibility of any consistent knowledge – or sense – of self. This may be one reason why transvestism is such a common element in the ritualistic, "self-losing" worship of orgiastic gods (see pp.54–9).

Cross-dressing has been an element of theatre at least since the Dionysian plays of ancient Greece (see p.56). Often, as in Elizabethan England, this was legally enforced as women were not allowed to appear on stage. In many cases, however, theatrical transvestism is aesthetically, or traditionally, preferred. For example, the "principal boy" in Western pantomime is invariably a woman, while the old woman, or "dame", is a man.

In Japanese Kabuki theatre, the women's roles are played by men, the onnagatas, *one of whom, Tamasaburo, from the troupe of the Kabukiza Theatre, Tokyo, is shown here. The* onnagata *is held up to Japanese women as someone to be emulated. The great 18th-century* onnagata *Yoshizawa Ayame declared that a woman could not express ideal feminine beauty, "for she could only rely on the exploitation of her physical characteristics, and therefore not express the synthetic ideal". Japanese audiences like to see the plays of Shakespeare performed with* onnagatas *in the female roles, as this makes the drama more artificial, and thus more skilful, and more beautiful.*

Orgy and possession

The sacred orgy breaks down or blurs the boundaries that define human beings as individuals, isolating them not just from each other but from the rest of nature, heaven and the gods. Orgies among the Marind Anim of southern New Guinea were designed to relive the primal moment of creation; during the orgy, according to the participants, the entire village becomes one being, with many heads, arms and legs. In merging chaotically with others, the self becomes amorphous and displaced. This can be an end in itself, as among the Marind Anim, or it can be a way of relinquishing a sense of self, so that some other force might take its place.

The ancient Greeks had two complementary notions: *enthousiasmos* (enthu-siasm), the state of being possessed by a god; and *ekstasis* (ecstasy), the state of being literally "beside oneself". Ecstasy did not guarantee enthusiasm, but was a necessary pre-condition for it, in order to make room for the possessing spirit. The Greeks knew that ecstasy could be induced by music, dancing, alcohol and sexual abandon; and all these elements were combined in the cult of Dionysos, a late addition to the Greek pantheon, whose worship was thought to have originated in Thrace or further east.

There were conflicting accounts of Dionysos's origins, but the most popular story was that he was the son of Zeus and a mortal woman called Semele. When Zeus, at Semele's request, revealed himself to her in his full glory,

The Banquet of the Gods *by H. van Balen the Elder (1575–1632). Ecstatic rituals were frequently an imitation of the behaviour of the gods, who are often portrayed in scenes of wild, sensual abandon.*

A Roman relief (2nd–4th century AD), showing a scene of Dionysian revelry, with the youthful Bacchus, or Dionysos (left), mounted on a leopard, and his companion Silenus (right) on a horse.

she was consumed in a ball of fire, and the god had to save the unborn Dionysos by enclosing him in his own thigh (a common euphemism for genitalia), until he was ready to be born.

Dionysos was a fertility god, specifically concerned with the vine, and wine-drinking was an important part of his ritual. The Greeks added many different ingredients to their wine, and it has been suggested that, at religious festivals, these included hallucinogenic substances such as wheat ergot (similar in its effects to LSD). At the great mystery of Demeter (see pp.16–19), such hallucinogens revealed visions to the worshippers, while at Dionysian festivals they helped induce the sexual frenzy of the orgy, as well as more directly invoking the ecstasy that the revellers sought. In early representations, Dionysos was an austere figure who did not seem to be

participating in his own celebrations, but he was later depicted as a drunken, effeminate or androgynous youth. His retinue (*thiasos*) included animals and mythical figures such as the lascivious satyrs, and lesser sexual gods such as Priapus or Pan.

Female revellers or followers of Dionysos were known as Maenads, or Bacchantes, and wore men's clothing. Cross-dressing is characteristic of sacred orgies, but, in contrast to the individual sacred transvestite (see pp. 48–53), this does not seem to be an attempt to embody the sum of both sexes in the self. Rather, it is another part of the orgiastic prescription of the blurring of all boundaries.

There were four main Dionysian festivals: the Rural Dionysia in December, the Lenaea in January, the Anthesteria in February and the month-long Great

RIGHT AND BELOW *These two 6th-century BC Greek vases show different aspects of Dionysian revelry. Copulating with animals (right) was often a part of the orgy; Dionysos's retinue contained many mythical animal or part-animal beings, such as the centaurs (half-human, half-horse), and the satyrs (half-human, half-goat). The descriptions of these beings may have arisen from accounts of Dionysian bestiality.*

RIGHT AND BELOW *These two 6th-century BC Greek vases show different aspects of Dionysian revelry. Copulating with animals (right) was often a part of the orgy; Dionysos's retinue contained many mythical animal or part-animal beings, such as the centaurs (half-human, half-horse), and the satyrs (half-human, half-goat). The descriptions of these beings may have arisen from accounts of Dionysian bestiality.*

Greek drama grew out of the Dionysian festival, and was originally itself a form of worship. The word "comedy" is derived from komos, *the dance of the Dionysian revellers. The satyr-actor (below) was an important character in early Greek drama, and even actors playing ordinary male roles used to wear grotesque artificial phalluses. The actor, like the ecstatic worshipper, must put aside his or her own personality in order to take up another.*

or City Dionysia beginning in March. They were apparently less concerned with fertility than with the release of sexual tensions, and the quest, quite literally, to lose oneself in the crowd. Most ritual orgies, however, have at least an element of sympathetic magic about them, designed to provoke nature into greater abundance. The three-day Greek *thesmophoria*, which took place every autumn to worship Demeter, was restricted to women, but involved symbolic copulation between notional phalluses (such as pine-cones and snakes) and the decaying bodies of piglets, which represented the female genitalia. The climax of the ritual involved specially purified women descending into the pit that held the piglets and bringing out the remains, which were sown with seeds (to be planted in the new year), and offered on the altar of Demeter.

The fertility orgy has survived into the 20th century in much of the world, although Christian missionaries, colonial authorities and national governments have gone a long way toward eradicating the practice. One Marind Anim initiation, now extinct, was a three-day orgy in which everybody except the initiates took part. At the end of the festival, a girl was brought forward to lie under a platform supporting heavy logs, and the initiates coupled with her one by one until, when the last

*The Holi festival of India –
seen here in Rajasthan –
survived as an orgiastic
fertility ritual during the years
of British colonial rule, but it
was under pressure from
reformers even then. Since
independence (1947), it has
been toned down by the
authorities, and now
resembles a Mardi Gras or
similar street celebration. The
participants throw red powder
or spray each other with red
liquid, which is a symbol of
sexual potency.*

initiate was with her, the supports of the platform were knocked away and the logs fell, killing them both.

Human sacrifice, sometimes planned as a fertility offering, but sometimes incidental to the ritual itself, is a frequent element in orgiastic worship. The Maenads, in their abandon, were said to disembowel men with their bare hands. When Dionysos was imported into Rome as Bacchus, guardians who wanted their young wards killed would send them to be "initiated" into the cult, confident that they would not survive the depradations enacted on them by the frenzied worshippers. The discovery of this practice led, according to the 1st-century BC Roman historian Livy, to the arrest of 7,000 Roman citizens.

The Dionysian festival found a place even in stricter religions, which recognized the need for an occasional

A NEW GUINEA SEANCE

Among the Gebusi of south-central New Guinea, a seance lasts all night, and may be used to find the cause of an illness, track down a sorcerer or find game. A young man becomes a spirit medium when he is told by an existing medium that a spirit woman desires and wants to marry him. During the seance, the medium's soul departs so that his body can be occupied by his spirit wife or her friends and relatives. The absent medium's spirit is meanwhile enjoying the delights of the spirit world, including feasts, dances and affairs with other spirit women. Because of such attractions, the role is eagerly embraced by Gebusi men, and mediums make up some fifteen per cent of the adult male population.

Women are not permitted to attend a Gebusi seance. The men maintain a constant stream of lewd songs and stories as a form of flirtation with the spirit woman, who must be kept amused throughout the seance to stop her flying away. At the same time, the presence of the often foul-mouthed, seductive spirit (a Gebusi ideal of feminine sexuality) stirs the pent-up sexual frustration of the men at the seance, strengthening it into the aggression that will be unleashed if game is located, or if a sorcerer is discovered and has to be hunted down and killed.

catharsis of the desires they so assiduously repressed. Elements of the Roman Saturnalia, which was characterized by unrestrained, orgiastic merrymaking, eventually became part of the celebrations of Christmas. Another festival, the Feast of Fools, or Feast of Asses, was condemned by the Council of Toledo as early as AD635, but was sanctioned by the medieval Church and continued to be popular in parts of Europe until the 17th century. The feast took place on January 11. Men and women swapped clothing or dressed up as minstrels or animals, and elected a bishop or a pope of fools to lead them in an Asses' Mass, at which everybody brayed throughout the service. Even the clergy paraded through the town, pelting people with dung and singing obscene songs. The sexual licence granted by the Feast is illustrated by a 15th-century ruling from the Chapter of Sens, in France, which requests (rather than demands) that those wishing to copulate should go outside the church to do so.

POSSESSION AND EXORCISM

Sexual feelings can often seem like powerful, alien beings, invading and even taking over the body and the mind. In *De Praestigiis Daemonum*, the first scientific study of possession, the German Dr de Weier (1515–76) noted that nuns claiming to be possessed all displayed the same sort of erotic convulsions. Attempts made to "cure" them through exorcism rarely worked; separating the nuns from the young men who excited their fantasies proved more successful. The relatively modern phenomenon of poltergeist activity – in which objects are moved or broken, apparently by a disturbed spirit – is, similarly, often traced to the presence in a household of a teenage child, denying or struggling to cope with a newly awakened sexuality.

Among the Tuareg of Niger, the women are occasionally possessed by spirits who bring illnesses of the heart, soul and liver – "the seat of all sentiments, especially love and anger". The exorcism of these spirits is a parody of Tuareg courtship: a public event, whose success depends upon the licentiousness of the men, who make advances to the women that would normally be considered insulting and unacceptable. Although the spirits are said to be passed from mother to daughter, the Tuareg women privately believe that possession is the sign of a secret love.

St Benedict Exorcizes a Devil from a Man Possessed *by Sodoma (1477–1549). Possession by demons was often considered to have a sexual basis.*

VOODOO

Voodoo is a cult that is characterized by spirit possession. The gods of western Africa survived in the memories of Haitian slaves as *loa*, spirit powers lying somewhere between the world of humans and the unapproachable supreme deity; some *loa* correspond to Roman Catholic saints, deriving from the period of French colonization in the 18th century. At voodoo ceremonies, the *loa* can be invoked for protection and guidance, or to cause harm by magic. They manifest themselves by possessing, or "mounting", the body of a celebrant, who has been prepared for the entrance of the god by a physically exhausting ritual that includes sacrifice, hypnotic drumming and uninhibited, ecstatic dancing. The person who has become possessed (the *gagnin loa*) is referred to as the *loa*'s horse, and any actions he or she performs are held to be the work of the god. The idea of humans as potential mounts of the gods is common to possession cults throughout Africa, and is shared with other Afro-Caribbean religions, such as Candomblé and Santeria.

To the voodoo faithful, it is impossible to be human and god at the same time, so for the *loa* to enter, the self must leave. Individuals who have been possessed will awake from a daze, not remembering anything they have said or done. Frequently, the

Voodoo celebrants dance in the graveyard at Port au Prince, Haiti, on All Saints' Day. They are mounted, or hoping to be mounted, by Ghede, the lord of eroticism and of the dead.

"mounting" is against the "horse's" will, and the body will twitch, thrash and grimace as the *loa* and the body's own spirit battle for its control. Many people may be mounted simultaneously by the same *loa*.

The trickster god of death and graveyards, Ghede, is especially popular among the poor, because of his love of mocking the powerful to their faces. Like other orgiastic gods, Ghede delights in confusing the sexuality of his followers, making the men dress as women and the women as

men; he may possess people of either sex. Ghede is also the phallic lord of eroticism, whose behaviour can range from sly suggestiveness to outright sexual assault. The freedom conferred by being possessed by Ghede creates a temptation to pretend to be mounted by him. Suspect possessions are tested by having rum sprayed into their open eyes and being offered crude rum steeped in twenty-one spices: although he is a sensual *loa*, Ghede, as lord of the dead, is also insensate, and the only one able to endure such trials.

The Order of the Soul

The history of any major religion is a complex mixture of inspiration, faith, mass appeal, political expediency, dogma, intolerance, propaganda and warfare. Every religion has at some time borrowed aspects of other religions, and absorbed elements of popular culture that ran counter to its teachings but proved too tenacious to wipe out and too powerful to ignore. It is not surprising that the echoes of archaic fertility and phallus-worshipping rituals should be found, however attenuated, in almost every surviving faith.

A common relic of the ancient perceived link between human beings and nature is the belief that an individual's sexual conduct can cause widespread harm, by offending a god or gods, who then punish the whole community. This vestigial archaism is one reason why most religions legislate on sexual behaviour. A faith's rich diversity of sexual rules may also arise from the discovery that some simple, ideal code – such as total abstinence – is not possible in practice, and needs to be modified with a painstakingly rationalized scheme of qualifications that more accurately reflect how its followers behave.

This chapter looks at sexual aspects of the major faiths, and should not be considered as an attempt to provide a comprehensive overview of the beliefs of a given religion.

Two Israelite couples depicted in bed in their tents, from an illustrated history of the Jews, c.1400. The 1st-century AD Jewish historian Josephus noted that "the Law recognizes no sexual connections, except the natural union of husband and wife, and that only for the procreation of children". Sexual behaviour is similarly subject to regulation in almost all religions.

Humans, gods and goddesses

Once the problematical first moment of creation has been dealt with (see pp.32–3), many theogonies go on to describe the first gods quarrelling, co-operating, fighting and filling the heavens with more gods by a process of recognizably human reproduction, with the occasional miraculous modification. Tales of rape, marriage, seduction and birth among the gods can frequently be traced back to the political or military machinations of the people who believed in them. For example, Isis, originally a minor goddess of the Nile town of Perehbet, was "married" to Osiris – the deity of the ruling clan in neighbouring Busiris – at the time when the two towns formed an alliance.

Charismatic leaders and ancestral hero-figures, such as Alexander the Great, could make their bid for divinity by claiming that a god had impregnated their mother. Political ambition, therefore, may also underlie the numerous tales of humans seduced by gods. The Greek god Zeus was especially partial to human women and

A Roman mosaic from 3rd-century AD Tunisia depicting Ganymede, a Trojan youth who was so beautiful that Zeus, besotted, changed into an eagle and carried him off to be his cup-bearer.

A 3rd-millennium BC Egyptian relief of King Unas suckled by a goddess. Pharaohs claimed to be descended from the gods, and emphasized their divine status by marrying incestuously – usually a divine prerogative.

adopted a bewildering variety of forms to pursue them. He came to Io as a cloud; to Danaë as a shower of gold; to Europa as a bull; and to Leda as a swan. Zeus's subterfuges not only helped him to escape the vigilance of his wife, Hera, but protected his mortal lovers, one of whom burst into flames when the god's full glory was revealed (see pp.54–5).

There are other dangers in the love of the gods. The ancient Sumerian *Epic of Gilgamesh* tells how Ishtar, the queen of heaven, attempted to seduce the hero-king Gilgamesh. But he rejected her angrily and reminded her of her previous human lovers, such as Ishallanu, whom she "changed into a blind mole deep in the earth, one whose desire is

*The Indian goddess Kali, seen in this 18th-century gouache from
Nepal, is one example of the worldwide pattern equating the
lover or mother with the devourer. The fierce form of the benign
Parvati, Kali is simultaneously desirable and terrifying.*

THE DEVOURING LOVE

Neolithic tombs in the Vallée du Petit Morin in
France contain reliefs of female figures, believed
to be goddesses, carved into the walls. The
multiple aspects of early goddesses embraced
mother and lover and also devourer: the giver
of life taking life back. One ingenious effort to
escape this cycle was that of Polynesian hero
Maui. Rather than passing out of the womb of

the goddess into life and then back into her
mouth (and death), Maui tried to win immortality by returning into the body of the lady of
darkness, Hine-nui-te-po, via her threatening,
snapping vagina. He was killed in the attempt.

Some Native American legends, such as
those of the Apache and Navajo, tell of women
with deadly, toothed vaginas, some of which
even walk about independently. Such figures
are usually tamed or slain by culture heroes.

---

always beyond his reach". Gilgamesh
asked Ishtar if the same fate did not
await him: to become one blinded by his
desire, but doomed never to attain its
object. The *Epic of Gilgamesh* implies
that such will be the fate of anyone who
worships the gods. Similarly, one of the
most popular voodoo deities is Erzulie,
a goddess of love unburdened by any

duties as a fertility figure, and beloved
precisely because she has no dealings
with this messy world, and is a perfect
object of aspiration. Yet men who are
"married" to Erzulie cannot take
another wife, because she is so jealous,
and spend almost all their time in a
state of sick, desperate longing until the
goddess mounts them again (see p.59).

Phallic worship

The phallus is only ever worshipped in a state of erection, when as fructifier and lifegiver it becomes an emblem of godhead. The erect phallus was a feature of paleolithic art, and was often juxtaposed with images of animals, although whether this was intended to signify it as the source of all life can only be conjectured. Certainly in Egypt by the time of Sesostris I (*c.*1900BC), the harvest god Min was represented as a hugely ithyphallic (permanently aroused) human figure, and was referred to as a bull rejoicing in the cow, as well as a husband impregnating his wife.

With his large, unambiguously pointing phallus, Min was also the god of roads, guide and protector of travellers, a role he shared with other phallic gods. The earliest images of the Greek god Hermes were piles of stones, called herms, which served as landmarks, each topped with a single large boulder. Later the herm evolved into a quadrangular block with the relief of a phallus and two testicles on its front surface. Hermes not only guided the living, but was the *psychopompos*, or guide of souls. Perhaps because signs and landmarks are often placed at boundaries, phallic gods popularly became guardian spirits, as in the case of the Japanese Dosojin. Thousands of these carved stone figures still exist, usually at the edges of rice

A Bronze Age rock-engraving from Bohuslan, Sweden, showing an aroused figure that may be a man or a god, among depictions of hunting and boats. Many cultures still equate the phallus with spears or other weapons (see pp.12–15).

Dosojins, such as this one from Kanagawa Prefecture, are both phallic figures and composite male/female deities, revealing the comprehensive generative powers ascribed to the phallus.

fields, where they ensure the fertility of the crop and act as "pass-not-place" deities, protecting the fields from trespassers and evil spirits. Another possible explanation for the identification of protective gods with gods of fertility is that the ability to make crops grow was considered worthless without the power to defend them.

There are at least remnants of phallic worship surviving in all religions. Conquerors and missionaries have tended to try replacing old or local gods with comparable figures from their own pantheons, and the original gods usually survive such appropriations in some form. Ascetic Buddhism attempted to absorb the Dosojin into the image of the *bodhisattva* Kisitigarbha, who had his "private parts drawn into a sheath": yet behind the statue of Kisitigarbha in the Buddhist temple at Nagoya, Japan, is a curtain hiding two carved phalluses, labelled Dosojin. The Aryan invaders of India who criticized the people they conquered for "having the phallus as a god" were within a few centuries worshipping the *linga* (phallus) of Shiva (see pp.68–9). There are phallic elements to the folk customs surrounding sacred trees, especially in Ireland, Mediterranean Europe and Japan.

In Christianity, phallic worship survived as "the enemy", in the figure of priapic, Pan-like Satan, as well as in the form of (often invented) priapic saints. For example, St Guignole, the first Abbé of Landevenec in France, became a phallic figure when his name was confused with the verb *gignere*, to engender; his chapel survived until 1740. The statues of such saints had exaggerated members, which were often

Priapus, the Greco-Roman god of gardens, in the form of a Roman oil-lamp dating from the 1st century AD. According to the Satires of Horace, Priapus scared off thieves by threatening them with "the crimson stick stretching from his obscene groin"; this lamp, emerging from the surrounding dark, would have been intended to startle intruders.

independently anointed and worshipped, and sometimes even used as magic dildos by women wishing to conceive (see pp.16–19).

St Augustine (AD354–430) bemoaned the "independent autocracy" of the penis, which acted against the personal will of its bearer. This wooden wind-charm phallus from Bhutan, hanging from the edge or corner of a building in the typical protective capacity of the phallic symbol, twists and turns in the wind with symbolic uncontrollability. A conscious loss of self-control has been encouraged in many rowdy phallic ceremonies from the Dionysian processions of ancient Greece (see pp.54–9) to traditional Japanese phallic festivals, such as the one that still takes place each April in Kawasaki.

ISIS AND OSIRIS

In Egyptian mythology, Osiris was, in varying accounts, a king or a god who brought civilization and the cultivation of crops to Egypt. He was killed by his brother Seth, and his body cut up and scattered so that his wife Isis (who was also his sister) had to spend many years gathering together the parts. But she was never able to find the penis, which had been thrown into the Nile, and so she fashioned a new one out of wood, which was so effective that she was able to use it to

conceive the god Horus. Isis also instituted rites in honour of Osiris. The Greek historian Herodotus, in the 5th century BC, described these as involving puppets, worked by strings and carried by women from village to village. Each puppet had a "male member moving and near as big as the rest of the body".

The myth, like those of other dead and resurrected gods or goddesses (see pp.16–19), reflects the awareness that new life springs from death. Osiris's original penis, by remaining in the underworld, turns the land of the dead into the eternal source of fertility.

China: ritual and regulation

Confucianism, Taoism (see pp.138–43) and Buddhism (see pp.70–71) have all waxed and waned in relation to each other as forces in Chinese religious thought and behaviour. They have also influenced each other, and at any time in the last 2,000 years, an individual would probably have lived according to more than one of them at the same time. From the time of the Han dynasty (202BC–AD220) until about the 12th century, it was common for people to regulate their public lives by Confucian principles and their private lives by Taoism.

Confucius (551–479BC) was more concerned with ethics than with mysticism. Perhaps for this reason, he is still honoured by the Chinese People's Republic (annual celebrations in his temple in Shantung were revived in 1957). He created an elaborate, ceremonial system for regulating society, based on the ideal of the well-ordered family – itself based on *hsiao* (filial piety). This was not merely restricted to the living: a man had a duty to all the past generations of his family – in effect, he was keeping them healthy in the afterlife – and an obligation to beget sons who would maintain this duty in the future. Daughters would not do: a women was regarded as irrevocably inferior to a man, and her only functions were to obey her husband and his parents, to look after the household and to bear healthy male children. In contrast to the Taoist, who sought a personal immortality, the Confucian aimed for immortality through reproduction.

To this end, Confucianism advocated polygamy. A middle-class householder might have between three and a dozen wives, a nobleman more than thirty, while the emperor was expected to have at least one queen, three consorts, nine second-rank and twenty-seven third-rank wives, and eighty-one concubines. These had to be slept with in the right order, with the right frequency, and according to rank. Secretaries kept records of who had been honoured, and of pregnancies and menstrual periods. It was essential that women should not substitute for each other; and by the 8th century, with seraglios comprising hundreds of women, the secretaries had taken to stamping the arm of each woman who had slept with the emperor. The stamp said, "Wind and moon [sexual union] are forever new", and was

Spring Morning in the Palace
by Ch'iu Ying (16th century).
A woman, probably one of a
nobleman's wives, sits for her
portrait, surrounded by other
female members of the household
– more wives, and concubines.

A late 19th-century painting of a couple in a tender erotic scene. Taoists did not share the Confucians' low opinion of women, and because Taoism and Confucianism were often practised side by side, couples were often more loving and considerate with each other in private than their public behaviour might suggest.

rubbed with cinnamon ointment to prevent it from washing off.

Confucianism disapproved of casual contact between the sexes, which might disrupt their carefully orchestrated polygamous timetables. Segregation rules were often very strict, and the second council of Macon, in AD 585, decreed that no male corpse be buried next to a female corpse that had not decomposed. Such strictures, however, were rarely adhered to.

Taoists were more concerned with the spiritual properties of semen than with its procreative functions, but they recognized the need to reproduce. To produce a healthy child, a man was advised to build up his male essence by copulating without ejaculation many times before attempting to impregnate his wife. A woman was considered most likely to conceive soon after menstruation. Any child conceived in daytime, at midnight, during a thunderstorm or an eclipse, or under a rainbow was thought to be in considerable danger.

When Buddhism arrived in China, traditionally around the 1st century AD, it came under attack from Confucians because its creed of celibacy was considered unnatural, and because it extended a greater spiritual respect to women. Buddhist nuns were taught to read and write, and renounced their sacred duty to produce male children. These nuns could come and go among the women's quarters, and became popular with Chinese women as confidants, messengers and advisers. During the T'ang dynasty (AD618–907) they were attacked, in a Confucian smear campaign, for supposedly performing unnatural acts, running brothels under the guise of nunneries, cooking love philtres and acting as go-betweens in illicit affairs.

Hinduism: asceticism and desire

Hinduism embraces both asceticism (*tapas*) and desire (*kama*): these are considered not necessarily as opposites, but as interchangeable forms of energy. One of the three major Hindu gods, Shiva, is an ascetic who is represented as a phallus, and who in some traditions continuously copulates in order to generate the universe (see pp.144–9). Although asceticism is praiseworthy, it can generate a dangerous amount of magic "heat", which may cause fires, droughts or earthquakes, and can threaten the gods themselves. Hindu myth abounds with stories illustrating this, such as that of the seer Vishvamitra and the beautiful nymph Menaka who was sent by the god Indra to tempt him and break the force of his austerities (see p.26).

Hindu marriage reflects these seemingly contradictory aspects. From the time of the Vedas (the central Hindu sacred texts, composed around the 1st millennium BC by the Aryan settlers of India), marriage was regarded as a sacrifice in itself. An unmarried man was called "one without a sacrifice", yet was at the same time described as only "a half man, and the second half is wife". Priests, as well as laymen, would marry, and vows of celibacy were usually for a

limited period. Of the vast number of possible ceremonies that may accompany a modern Hindu marriage, many involve the bride and groom representing Shiva and his consort in their joint aspects as ascetics and glorious deities: the groom, for example, might wear a loincloth and a crown of gold or silver paper.

Many Hindu ideas linking the gods and sexuality may go back to the Indus civilization that reached its peak *c*.2000BC. Archeologists have uncovered seals showing an ithyphallic, three-faced god, known as the proto-Shiva. Terracotta statues of naked women may represent a mother goddess who became Parvati or Kali.

Sensual sculpture, such as this 13th-century carving, is a feature of Hindu art.

The sacred philosophical texts the Upanishads include descriptions of ritual sex, anticipating the development of Tantra (see pp.144–55). The first Upanishad stresses the mystical importance of semen (see pp.40–45); in the second, sexual intercourse is given the status of a liturgical chant. The epic poems, such as the *Mahabharata*, are almost as sacred as the Vedas, and are more accessible. They describe four human ideals or objects: duty or virtue (*dharma*), gain (*artha*), love (*kama*) and salvation (*moksha*). *Dharma* is usually seen as underlying all the other ideals, but in the more popular parts of the *Mahabharata*, *kama* is the innermost core of the world, the womb of both *dharma* and *artha*.

INFLUENCES OF COLONIZATION

Hindu eroticism has often suffered at the hands of invaders. In one year, the 17th-century Muslim Mughal ruler Aurangzeb destroyed more than 200 temples containing images of naked or cavorting figures. The most powerful repressive influence on Hinduism was British Victorian prudery, whose morals and aesthetics, often adopted wholesale by educated Hindus, were perpetuated long after the end of colonial rule (see pp.26–9).

Krishna – the eighth avatar (incarnation) of Vishnu, the Preserver – is one of the most popular of the major Hindu deities. A famous warrior, he is also mischievous, charming and a god of love. In one famous story, Krishna lures the gopis *(cowgirls) to him by playing his flute in a forest glade, driving them wild with desire. By multiplying himself he manages to satisfy 900,000* gopis *simultaneously.*

Krishna's favourite gopi *is Radha, and their romance inspired a body of* bhakti *(devotional) poetry that became a focus for popular worship, often mocking the staid Vedic rituals of the* brahmins *(priestly caste). Scenes from the story of the seduction of the* gopis *are a frequent subject of illustration and feature an often exquisite sensuality. This painting in the Pahari style shows Krishna watching from a tree as the* gopis *bathe.*

SHIVA *LINGA*

One of the most common objects of veneration in India is the *linga* (phallus; see also pp.64–5). Worshipped as the incarnation of Shiva, the *linga* represents the erotic side of his dual nature, the aspects of fertility and re-creation. Because Shiva always retains his seed, the *linga* is always erect, full of potential creation. The Hindu worship of phallic objects can probably be traced back 4,000 years to phallic cone-shaped objects found in the Indus Valley.

One Hindu legend tells how Shiva went to the forest in order to revive his sexual powers through asceticism. Wandering through the forest naked, ithyphallic (continu-ously erect) and dancing, he attracted the wives of the local sages, who fell in love with him. The sages cursed his *linga*, and made it fall to the ground, but it caused a huge fire and grew immeasur-ably tall, so that even the gods Brahma and Vishnu could not find its top or bottom. Shiva only stopped the flames after the sages agreed to worship his phallus.

As in this 5th-century example from central India, an image of Shiva is often carved on one side of a linga, *forming a connection between the personified and the iconic forms of the deity.*

Buddhism: discipline of the body

Although Buddhism as a religion seeks to escape the torments and temptations of continual rebirth into the life of the flesh, the early Buddhist stories, told by celibate monks, sometimes contain detailed physical description. When the future Buddha was born, he bore on his body the marks of a great man, one mark being that his penis, "that part of the blessed one that ought to be hidden", was "enclosed in a sheath". The Buddha's mother is described as "radiant, alluring … whose belly, with its bright streak of downy hair, curves like the palm of the hand".

As a young man the future Buddha was married and fathered a child, but he left his wife and son in order to seek enlightenment (*nirvana*), never returning. The doctrine of the Middle Way is the formula for a moderate life lived between the extremes of sensuality and self-torturing asceticism; it prescribes celibacy as part of a general rejection of all forms of craving. Buddhist monks were taught to meditate on the body as a heap of bones, and sex was denounced as animal. Women were considered to

An 18th-century bronze of the Tantric Buddha Hevajra and his shakti *(female principle), in Tantric embrace. In Tantric Buddhism, ritual sex is a means of attaining transcendence.*

be dangerous; several legends tell of the Buddha's reluctance to allow women into the Buddhist order; he denied his aunt three times before admitting her at the request of his chief disciple, warning that Buddhism would last only half as long as it would have done if women had been excluded.

The *Vinaya Pitaka*, or "discipline basket" governing Theravada Buddhism

---

THE NAKED FAITH

Jainism is a religion that arose at the same time as Buddhism, with similar doctrines of reincarnation and the attainment of *nirvana* by abandoning all ties. In principle, if not usually in practice, Jainism is even stricter than Buddhism in its renunciation of the flesh. Jain monks – the only people who could even theoretically attain *nirvana* – were originally expected to become

Digambaras – "sky-clad" – and go everywhere naked. Some modern Jains still adhere to this precept.

An erotic carving from a 10th–11th-century temple at Khajuraho, Madhya Pradesh. Despite Jain asceticism, their art is often highly sensual, influencing the iconography of Tantra. A third of the temples of Khajuraho are Jain, decorated with sportive, naked figures similar to those of their Hindu neighbours.

THE BIRTH OF THE BUDDHA

The earliest accounts of the future Buddha's birth stress his noble ancestry, and the portentous dreams had by his mother when she was pregnant, but otherwise present it as a normal event. Later legends introduce elements of miraculous non-sexuality. In these, the future Buddha

An 11th-century mural from Ladakh showing the Buddha's mother dreaming (left) that an elephant enters her womb (a symbol of her conception) and (right) giving birth: the future Buddha emerges from her right side.

entered his mother's womb unaided, after she spent a night away from her husband. She gave birth not sitting or lying, like other women, but standing up, and in some

narratives died seven nights later, before she slept with her husband again, "because it is not fitting that she who bears a peerless one should afterward indulge in love".

(the older, Southeast Asian, form of Buddhism), said that it was better for a monk's *linga* (phallus) to enter a snake or a fire than to enter a woman's *yoni* (vagina). The *Vinaya* prohibits masturbation and most forms of contact between men and women, often showing great ingenuity in its construction of possible scenarios. One story, to illustrate the principle that it is acceptable to emit semen when asleep but not when awake, concerns a monk who is dozing by the roadside. Noticing that he has an erection, a succession of passing women lie with him, but because he does not wake up he is considered guiltless, despite gaining a local reputation as "a bull among men". Prohibitions extended to handling, or even sleeping under the same roof as, female animals. And if a monk's mother fell into a ditch, he could offer her a stick to pull her out, but not his hand.

Despite such regulations, it was only brotherhoods of monks who were expected to be celibate. Lay Buddhists should try to live as chastely as they could, and hope to be reincarnated as monks in their next life. Gradually, especially in northern India, even the monks began to question whether a sex life really sabotaged their spiritual ambitions. By AD500, there were married monks in Kashmir, and the 8th-century founder of Buddhism in Tibet, Padmasambhava, had several wives. Tantric Buddhism (see pp.144–55), which developed in Tibet and northern India, also contributed to an increase in the number of married priests. In China and Japan, the solitary priests who officiated in Buddhist temples were frequently married, while monks living in communities tended to be celibate. Celibacy remains the norm for monks in much of Asia today.

Judaism: marriage and ancient beliefs

An illustration from a Jewish manuscript (c.1350). The rod of Aaron turns into a snake and swallows the snakes of the pharaoh's magicians: an episode that may be seen as emphasizing the phallic strength of Yahweh.

The Hebrew Scriptures describe practices that seem to be relics of ancient sex cults and phallic religions, from which Judaism gradually turned away. Despite the association of prostitution with the worship of foreign idols (see pp.24–9), King Rehoboam, the son of Solomon, tolerated the existence of male sacred prostitutes. Phallus-shaped rocks and pillars are described as sacred, and Moses worked magic with a rod that turned into a snake, a common phallic symbol. The Hebrews still burned incense to a brazen snake, made by Moses, in the 7th century BC. At least one phallic element survives into modern Judaism: circumcision, a sign of the covenant between man and God, has also been explained as a symbolic

human sacrifice; the use of flint knives to perform the ceremony in the stories of Moses and Joshua suggests the extreme antiquity of the custom.

The phallic snake – which, some Near Eastern peoples believed, instructed humans in sexual intercourse – first appears in the Bible tempting Eve, but Jewish commentators did not interpret the Fall as a demonstration of the evils of sex. Adam and Eve slept together only after they had left Eden: their original sin was simply disobedience of God. The first humans were told to "be fruitful and multiply", and Jews, like Muslims, are opposed to celibacy. Jewish lore states that sex, within marriage and for the purpose of procreation, should

The Cabbalistic Sefirot Tree, from Theatrum Hieroglyphicum *(1654) by Athanasius Kircher. During the 12th and 13th centuries, the mystical tradition of Cabbalism expanded the ancient Hebrew concept of* shekinah *(indwelling), which had originally signified the presence of God on earth, but came to be worshipped as "the wife of the king". The* shekinah *(represented at the base of the diagram) was the feminine power of the divine, and its relationship with God was described as the archetypal sexual union.*

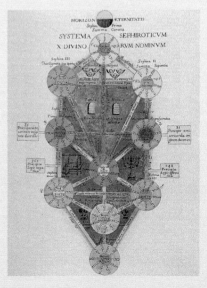

THE SONG OF SOLOMON

The Song of Solomon is a sensual, rapturous lyric, which makes no mention of Yahweh (God), and is closest in spirit to the Indian love lyrics of Krishna and Radha (see pp. 68–9). Probably a compilation or cycle of ancient folk-songs, it takes the form of a dialogue between two lovers, who address each other as equals. Its place in the canon of Jewish scripture was violently debated until AD100, when the rabbinical synod of Jamnia decided that it was an allegory of the relationship between God and Israel, referred to throughout the Hebrew Scriptures as a marriage. For the Jews and for the Christians who followed them in confirming the Song of Solomon as sacred scripture, the erotic language symbolized the relationship between the human and the divine. The English Authorized Bible went to great lengths to interpret the Song of Solomon spiritually. Phrases such as "lips like a thread of scarlet" and "breasts like two young roes" are said to refer to "the graces of the Church"; "his lips like lilies ... his belly as bright ivory" is "a description of Christ by his graces".

"Who is she that looketh forth as the morning, far as the morn ..."

be enjoyed; indeed, in some branches of Judaism, sex is considered a blessed duty to be carried out the evening before every Sabbath. The Torah (the first five books of the Hebrew Scriptures) places no limit on the number of a man's wives; the Talmud (Jewish lore and commentaries) sanctions four, specifying that each wife should sleep with her husband at least once a month.

Judaic tradition is correspondingly harsh on sexual practices that would not result in children; the book of Leviticus decrees the death sentence for homosexuality. Children had to be born inside marriage, and their paternity assured: adulterers should be put to death, and brides who could not prove their virginity might be stoned to death. The Hebrew Scriptures contain innumerable regulations about modesty, sexual cleanliness and marriage. Important customs surround a woman's menstruation: for a set time before and after, as well as during, her period, a wife abstains from sex. She then takes a ritual bath (*mekveh*) and, thus purified, goes to her husband. As a corollary, the element of abstention is said to increase sexual desire between husband and wife.

Early Christianity: celebration and moderation

Christianity began as a celebratory religion. The New Testament extends the Judaic concept of a marriage between God and his people, using the language of the bridegroom coming to take his bride that is found in the Dead Sea Scrolls. In the gospel of Mark, Jesus is asked why his disciples do not fast, when the disciples of John the Baptist and of the Pharisees do. Jesus answers, "Can the children of the bridechamber fast, while the bridegroom is with them?" Jewish custom prescribed fasting as a preparation for the Sabbath and feast days, but with the coming of Jesus, say the gospels, the marriage feast had already begun, and it would not end. The wedding imagery is so strong that the Catholic theologian and mystic Odo Casel (1896–1948) described baptism as the "bridal bath of the church".

Through his sympathetic responses to Mary Magdalene and the woman taken in adultery, Jesus is seen in the New Testament as much more open-minded than his contemporaries. Nonetheless, his observation that whoever looked lustfully upon a woman had already committed adultery with her in his heart was more rigorous than anything in the rabbinical tradition: suddenly, thoughts, not only acts, could be sinful. The militant asceticism of later Christianity is usually traced to the apostle Paul, who saw himself as a "best man" with the job of presenting his congregation "as a chaste virgin to Christ".

Paul was immersed in the mystery religions of Greece and the East, and it was probably he who introduced the tradition of the Eucharist, with its echoes of mystery rites in which the body of the god is ingested. He had an almost Dionysian sense of the relationship between body and spirit (see pp. 54–9), but shaped by a personal distaste for sex. In a letter to the Christian community at Corinth, Paul scolded: "Do you not know that bodies are members of Christ? Shall I therefore take the

Detail from The Marriage Feast at Cana *(1562) by Paolo Veronese. Jesus and Mary occupy the seats of the bridal couple (see also p.89).*

GNOSTICISM

As Christianity spread in the last years of the Roman Empire, it absorbed ideas from other, older creeds, while appearing to refute them. Its attitude to sexuality was influenced by Gnosticism and Manichaeism, both of which taught that the flesh was inherently evil, and by the Severians who believed that woman was created by the Devil – who also made man from the waist down.

The Gnostics, who flourished until the 4th century AD, believed the material body to be a prison, from which the soul was liberated when the light of wisdom (*gnosis*) planted its seed in the soul, making it the bride of the godhead (or, in the post-Christian Gnostic texts, of Jesus). Gnosis could be approached through either asceticism, or extreme licentiousness, which, by overloading the body's senses, stripped them of the hold they otherwise had on the soul. As a result, despite its rejection of the flesh, the influence of Gnosticism on Christianity was subtle and ambivalent (although Gnostics were branded heretics); and its eroticism reappears in the language of the Christian love mystics (see pp.86–7).

The Magdalene *by Correggio (c.1489–1534).
In several Gnostic creeds, Mary Magdalene was
secretly educated by Jesus in the arts of love.*

members of Christ and make them members of a prostitute? God forbid. Do you not know that he who joins himself to a prostitute becomes one body with her? For as it is written, 'The two shall become one flesh'. But he who is joined with the Lord is one spirit."

Paul also censured the puritans at Corinth who shunned all earthly pleasures, and advised that married couples should not deny each other sex, except for an agreed, limited period to enrich their spiritual lives. But he believed that marriage was always a second-best option – the resort of those who did not have his own "gift" for celibacy, which was superior as it did not interpose anyone else between oneself and God.

THE LOVE FEAST

The Eucharist – the sacrament commemorating the Last Supper, in which the body of Christ is symbolically eaten, in the form of bread and wine – did not become the major Christian ritual until the 4th century. It was preceded by the *agape*, or love feast, a real meal in which sexual differences were forgotten, and men and women greeted each other with a kiss of peace before undergoing a collective ecstatic experience.

Communities grew up, called *agapetae*, that were based on this sense of universal love, although different communities had very different approaches to its physical expression. The Carpocratians are said to have had sex with each other indiscriminately, while the men of the Valesians castrated themselves, both to remove the temptation of lust and to emphasize their similarity to the women.

Islam: marriage and mysticism

Islam combines elements of Judaic, Christian and early Arab attitudes to sexuality. In one account of the birth of Islam, sex plays a crucial role as a litmus test of divine authenticity. When the Prophet Muhammad received his first vision of the angel Gabriel and was struck with wonder, his wife Khadija sent her servants to bring him back to her. He "sat by her thigh and drew close to her", and when he announced that he could still see the angel, Khadija made him "come inside her shift"; Gabriel departed at once, proving by his modesty that he was an angel and not a demon. A later story states that men should avoid being naked, as the recording angels are always present except when men are excreting or engaged in sexual intercourse.

The Prophet is said to have declared that "the whole world is to be enjoyed, but the best thing in the whole world is a good woman". He disliked celibacy, and "there is no monkery in Islam". Nevertheless, ritual abstinence is enjoined during the daylight hours of Ramadan (the month of fasting), and during the whole of a pilgrimage to Mecca. Sex is encouraged by the Qur'an, providing it is preceded by an act of piety, after which, men are told, "your women are like furrows to you, so come to your tillage as you wish". The harsh Islamic rules against various sexual practices (such as the stoning to death of married fornicators) come from the Traditions (stories and customs surrounding the actions of the Prophet) rather than the Qur'an itself.

Muhammad himself had a number of wives. One of the most often quoted verses of the Qur'an decrees: "Marry

The private pleasure of Prince Muhammad Shuja (c.1678–98), by the Mughal painter Hunhar. The style of Mughal erotic paintings was greatly influenced by Hindu erotic art.

such of the women as seems good to you; two, or three, or four … if you fear that you may not be fair [to several wives], then take only one." This has been taken as licensing, or limiting, a man to four wives, but has also been quoted in support of monogamy, since no man but the Prophet could be "fair" to more than one woman.

Parts of the Qur'an state that believing men, women and children will enter Paradise as families, but other verses describe only the delights of men, who will be waited on in Paradise by houris: bright-eyed maidens with swelling breasts, "amorous and of equal age".

Among the Islamic Sufi mystics, the 12th-century writer Ahmad al-Ghazali

WORKS OF FANTASY

The word harem meant "forbidden", and derived from the Arabic *haram*, which also meant "sacred". The harem was forbidden specifically to other men, and those of the caliphs of Baghdad were jealously guarded places. The lack of any real information about what went on inside fuelled countless over-heated imaginations, and led to romantic fantasies ranging from the *Arabian Nights* to the odalisque paintings of Ingres or Matisse.

The woman of the harem was a mystery; her beauty, wit and charm were the subject of endless speculation. By the 8th century, the harem had inspired a new kind of poetry, in which the beloved's unattainability was one more facet of her imagined perfection. Poets of the time, such as Djamil, extolled the subjection of the lover to the beloved, although it made him die by inches, "weeping for love of his assassin". This chaste desire expanded into the concept of "pure" love (see pp.112–13), and may have influenced the troubadours (see pp.84–5).

taught that God was beauty, and beauty was intrinsically lovable, while the great 13th-century poet, Djalal al-Din Rumi, described his quest for the Beloved ("who comes like a thief in the night") in hundreds of verses. Farid al-Din Attar, in the 13th century, wrote of the state in which the self has vanished in the Beloved. Yet the idea of union with God was and is abhorrent to most orthodox Muslims, who consider that there is an infinite distance between themselves and the deity. The sexual symbolism of the Sufis is closer to the allegorical bridal mysticism of their Christian contemporaries (see pp.86–7) than to the sacramental sex of Taoism or Tantra (see pp.138–43, 144–55).

Sudanese Beja women with their faces veiled. The veil was originally adopted in Islam by the wives of the Prophet, anxious to escape the insults of non-believers in the street. Islamic justification for veiling women is not only to protect their modesty, but also to shield men from their dangerous sexuality.

The Wounded Body: Sex in the West

It is impossible to overestimate the influence of the Christian Church on Western sexuality. Even those in the West who have tried to forge a new sexual morality – from the Marquis de Sade to Sigmund Freud – have always done so against a background established according to a Christian agenda.

Much of what the Western world considers to be sinful has little to do with religious scripture. The catalogue of sexual sins was largely invented by a small number of men living through the last years of the Roman Empire (*c*.4th–5th centuries AD) – the Fathers of the Church. In order to subdue their sensual desires, they turned to asceticism and celibacy, validating such practices with theological arguments, which were subsequently disseminated and enforced by an ever more powerful Church. Although many people now see such self-denial as arising from an exaggerated or unhealthy contempt for the flesh, these early saints were motivated by an intense concentration on the spirit and a determination to attain greater purity and closeness to God.

A panel from the 9th-century Grandval Bible, depicting the story of the temptation and fall of Adam and Eve and their expulsion from the Garden of Eden. The "original sin" of Adam and Eve was disobedience, leading to the acquisition of forbidden knowledge. It was St Augustine who linked original sin with sexuality and the spirit's inability to control the flesh – an interpretation that had a powerful effect on Christian moral teaching, although it was never universally accepted by the Church.

The classical world

The ancient Greeks created gods who can be seen as acting out their own unconscious fears and desires, and whom they could thus use to explain or justify extremes of their own behaviour. Plato said that "the greatest blessings come to us through madness, when it is sent as a gift of the gods", and "divinely inspired" manias ranged from epilepsy to love. In order to experience a god-given madness, the Greeks probably took hallucinogenic drugs, similar to LSD; they certainly used trance-inducing music, dancing, alcohol and sexual abandon (see pp.54–9), and experimented with anything that might bring about an awareness of the divine.

The gods of early Rome were much more abstract – symbols of moral behaviour, or protective principles such as Vesta (see p.20), which had no bodily form at all. It was only under Greek influence that the Roman gods became more recognizably human. For example, the Roman Liber, a patron of growth, became associated with the Greek Priapus, and the agricultural goddess Venus took on many characteristics of the Greek goddess of love, Aphrodite. By the late 1st century BC, Roman religion had become closely identified with the state, and removed from personal mystical concerns. As the empire became more unstable, people turned increasingly to

The fertility god Priapus weighing his penis, a fresco from Pompeii.

PROSTITUTES AND MATRONS

The *hetairai* – the most highly paid and well-respected prostitutes of ancient Greece – often performed religious duties for a fee. They were

hired to carry model phalluses through the streets of Athens in the festivals of Dionysos (see pp.54–7), and when the Persian king Xerxes attacked Greece, the temple *hetairai* of Corinth offered up the state's prayers and sacrifices. But their main concerns were secular: entertaining men and earning large profits for doing so. The Athenian orator Demosthenes (384–322BC) considered that *hetairai* brought pleasure, while wives were simply to provide "legitimate children and look after the housekeeping".

Hetairai were allowed the education and social privileges that were denied to wives. Treated as equals in an overwhelmingly masculine world, they were role models for generations of later, Roman, wives who attained a level of independence rare in the ancient world. By 195BC, Roman women were so confident and well organized that they would publicly mob tribunes in order to get laws changed.

A prostitute carrying a giant phallus, depicted on a Greek vase dating from 470BC.

A Roman wall painting depicting a Dionysian scene of orgiastic revelry.

ecstatic, often orgiastic, eastern religions. Roman religious fervour was also exacerbated by large numbers of independent-minded, wealthy women, who were excluded from public life or meaningful work. Such women turned to the spiritual (and often physical) comforts of cult religions, such as the Bacchus (Dionysos) worship imported from Greece.

Rome was a natural home for cult faiths, many of which were brought back along with foreign slaves taken in the empire's wars of conquest. The Phrygian goddess Cybele (see pp.38–9) had been adopted by Rome even before the arrival of Bacchus, in response to a prophecy that the invader Hannibal (3rd century BC) would be defeated if a great goddess were brought to the city. The Cybele cult mirrored the growth and degeneration of the empire. At first it was relatively innocuous, but, along with the increasingly barbaric spectacles of the Colosseum games, the cult became more bloodthirsty and orgiastic. Its growing extremism also reflected an attempt to hold on to worshippers who were being lured away by "new" divinities such as Isis, Mithras, Serapis and the Christian God.

Some of these cults were quickly curtailed by the Roman authorities. After a notorious scandal (see p.57), a Senate decree of AD186 banned the public worship of Bacchus except by special permission; and in AD19, the priests of Isis were executed after a matron was raped in the temple of Isis by a man pretending to be the god Anubis.

Christianity was the only Roman cult to survive with a large following, after the emperor Constantine adopted it as the official religion of the empire in the 4th century. Constantine's choice of faith was probably politically motivated: the well-organized Christian Church represented the best administrative tool available for holding together the fragmenting empire. As a result of this decision, Christianity became one of the greatest influences on human behaviour that the Western world has known.

A 2nd-century AD mosaic from Italy, depicting a dwarf in the act of sodomy. Sex-shows of great inventiveness and, often, brutality were as much a part of the spectacle at the Roman games as the slaughter of animals and the gladiatorial contests.

Denial of the flesh

Asceticism (from Greek *askesis*, exercise, training) can be found in all religions, but is more important in some (such as early Christianity and classical Jainism) than in others (such as Confucianism and Shinto). It typically involves celibacy, fasting, poverty, seclusion and, often, a degree of self-mortification, in a program of self-discipline and self-denial intended to achieve a spiritual goal, which varies from faith to faith (see pp.116–19). Even within Christianity, ascetics had differing aims: some were divorcing themselves from the material world, some were performing penance, and others were attempting to share the sufferings of Christ.

The early Fathers of the Church were not natural ascetics: they were men – often with active sex lives – tormented by the strength and uncontrollability of their desires. St Augustine (AD354–430) prayed, "Give me chastity ... but not yet." His contemporary, St Jerome, related how, when he was fasting in the desert, "I ... fancied myself among bevies of girls ... My mind was burning with the cravings of desire, and the fires of lust flared up from my flesh that was as that of a corpse."

Jerome called sex unclean, the theologian and moralist Tertullian (b.*c*.AD155) called it shameful, and St Ambrose (*c*.AD339–97) called it a defilement. For Augustine, it was specifically the loss of self-control that was so disturbing.

St Jerome by Leonardo da Vinci (1452–1519). Self-flagellation became part of the Christian tradition of the mortification of the flesh. In the 4th century, flagellation was considered the most effective form of penance, but by the 14th century, wandering bands of flagellants claimed that it was the only true way to salvation.

Writing about the Garden of Eden, he exclaimed, "Perish the thought that there should have been any unregulated excitement, or any need to resist desire!" God had given humans a blameless physical instinct designed to reproduce the species: it was the appetite and frenzy of lust that made sex shameful, and as all humans were procreated in a spirit of lust, the original sin of Adam and Eve was transmitted from generation to generation.

Procreation within marriage was the only acceptable goal of sex. Penitentials (books listing misdeeds and penalties) from the 6th to 9th centuries reveal that contraception was almost as sinful as murder, requiring penances lasting two to fifteen years. Even *coitus interruptus* – the only form of contraception sanctioned by the modern Roman Catholic Church – was a sin, but it attracted

The Temptation of St Anthony *by Jan Brueghel (1568–1625)*.

lighter penalties than oral or anal sex or the use of "poisons creating sterility". The Church also attempted to limit the days on which a married couple could try to procreate. Sex was made illegal on Sundays, Wednesdays and Fridays; for forty days before Easter and Christmas; and for three days before communion. It was forbidden when performing a penance, and during the time from conception to forty days after parturition.

Some of the Church Fathers even had doubts about procreation. For them, the injunction in the Hebrew Scriptures to be fruitful and multiply had been intended to establish a pool of the faithful from whom the Messiah might arise: as he had arisen, it was no longer valid. Jerome tolerated marriage because it peopled the world with virgins, who were held to be the brides of Christ.

CLERICAL CELIBACY

The celibacy of its priesthood has been a much debated issue in the Christian Church. One of the first authentic papal decrees, by Pope Sircius in AD386, tried with little success to prevent deacons from having sex with their wives. It was not until the 11th century that the papacy was sufficiently strong for Gregory VII to issue a complete prohibition on clerical marriage. It was already impossible for a man to marry after ordination, but married men could be ordained (many entered the Church as the only route to a professional career).

Gregory's prohibition caused an outcry, but he stirred up the laity to riot against married clergy, and to boycott any Mass taken by a recalcitrant priest. After an often bloody struggle, the principle of clerical celibacy was established. Today, the Catholic Church still demands celibacy of its priests, while the Protestant and the Eastern Churches allow married clergy. In the Greek Churches celibacy is thought appropriate only for bishops.

Troubadours and courtly love

A scene from the early 15th-century Très Riches Heures du Duc de Berry *by the Limbourg brothers, showing courtly figures near the castle.*

King Guilhem of Aquitaine is said to have invented the idea of courtly love at the beginning of the 12th century, when his habitual adultery was threatened by the success of the preacher Robert D'Abrissel in persuading the ladies of the court that the fires of hell lay in wait for adulterers. Guilhem responded with a series of poems, probably based on Arab prototypes (see pp.76–7), which argued that love was not a sin but a divine mystery, and that the woman who inspired love was a goddess worthy of adoration. This brilliant counter-attack was apparently successful.

The theme of ennobling love became popular with the wandering singers, poets and entertainers of the time. However, many of their clients were married noblewomen, and most of their songs were in the first person, which led to numerous problems, such as misunderstandings with the ladies and clashes with their husbands. In addition, it had long been an offence, sometimes punishable by death, to address a love-song to a married woman, as this was considered a kind of enchantment. It was a sternly moralistic entertainer called Macabru who solved the problem, by claiming that beauty and nobility alone were not enough to make a woman into a goddess: she must also possess virtue. She must, by definition, be unattainable.

From this innovation sprang the troubadours, a group of poets who each chose the wife of a feudal lord as the object of his affections, and dedicated all his poetry to her. A troubadour did not want to possess his lady (whom he called Mi-dons, My Lord). For most it was enough to see her, or be given some token from her, such as a glove. Even those who spoke of undressing their mistresses never mentioned consummation. The willingness of the lord to support his wife's troubadour, and even ennoble him, suggests that there was little suspicion or thought of adultery.

The troubadour movement quickly spread to northern France, Germany and England. Its rules were elaborated in 1186 by one Andrew, a chaplain at the court of Eleanor of Aquitaine. Courtly love, he wrote, "goes so far as the kiss and the embrace and the modest contact with the nude lover, omitting the final solace, for that is not permitted to those who wish to love purely". For the relief of sexual tension, Andrew advised the seduction of lower-class women, who would not inspire such an emasculating sense of awe. The troubadours thought of love as the union of hearts and minds, and not of bodies: it was the source of all good and virtue, because no man would do anything to lower himself in the eyes of his mistress.

The legacy of the troubadours comprises almost the whole of romantic literature, and a concept of chivalrous honour that had not existed in the West since the pederasty of the Greeks (see pp.46–7). Before the troubadours, knightly behaviour was barbaric and bloodthirsty. It was only when desire for a woman's approval became the motive for valour that what is now understood as chivalry came into being, if only as an ideal. Even the word "gentle" has been expanded by the troubadours' influence from its original sense of "well-born".

Tristan and Iseult by J. M. Strudwick (1849–1937). In the original story, the pair had an adulterous affair: their love became chaste and hopeless only as part of the romance tradition.

THE CATHARS

The religious movement of the Cathars, or "pure ones", appeared in Provence and Languedoc at the same time as the troubadours. The Cathars stressed sexual abstinence, and full initiates were not even supposed to sleep with their wives. They believed that the spirit had become trapped in the flesh, and that the avoidance of any fleshly pleasures helped to speed its escape. Because they were so confident of their own purity, men and women shared the same lodgings, which led the orthodox Church to accuse them of

immorality. Their abstinence, and consequent childlessness, also led to accusations that they engaged in anal sex, and because they were thought to be a sect that had entered France from Turkey via

The Dominicans introduced the rosary as a weapon to win back the image of the Virgin Mary into the control of the orthodox Church, after she had been adopted as a patron by sects preaching the possibility of chaste love. These sprang up at the same time as the Cathars and, like them, were branded heretical.

Bulgaria, the term *bougre*, a corruption of Bulgar, became a synonym for sodomite. The Cathars were mercilessly exterminated in the Albigensian crusades of the early 13th century.

The love mystics

The Christian love mystics, both men and women, imagined their souls as brides, and Christ as the bridegroom. Although mainstream Church doctrine advocated a suppression of sensuality, they also experienced visions in which the relationship was consummated.

One of the earliest and most influential was St Bernard of Clairvaux, who was born in AD1093. Bernard, like most love mystics, was greatly influenced by the *Song of Solomon* (see p.73), whose imagery he often borrowed. He preached that "if anyone once receives the spiritual kiss of Christ's mouth, he seeks eagerly to have it again and again". This first involved prostrating oneself to kiss Christ's feet, and then

working to become worthy to kiss his hand. For Bernard, the approach to God was a long apprenticeship in love, involving an increasingly sensitive heart and greater self-knowledge. He distinguished four ascending kinds of love: self-love; love of God for selfish ends; love of God for God's sake; and, curiously even higher than this, self-love for God's sake. "Love is the very being of the Bride," preached Bernard. "She is full of it, and the Bridegroom is satisfied with it. He asks nothing else."

No matter how far the soul progressed, it could never experience God completely, but only to the limits of its own capacity. Bernard wrote, "A curious explorer, I have plumbed my own

ABELARD AND HÉLOÏSE

The philosopher Peter Abelard (1079–1142) is remembered mainly for his tragic love affair with his student, Héloïse. Her uncle, a canon of Notre Dame cathedral, found out about their affair, and forced them into marriage. Having borne Abelard a son, Héloïse eventually denied the marriage and ran away to a convent, thinking to spare him the scandal. But the uncle thought that Abelard had sent her for the sake of his own reputation, and had men break into his room and castrate him. Abelard decided that this was just punishment

for his sins. He became a wandering teacher for the rest of his life, always avoiding Héloïse, who never stopped sending him passionate declarations of her love.

However, Abelard was also one of the inventors of

An 18th-century painting by Angelica Kauffman depicting Abelard presenting Hymen (the personification of marriage) to Héloïse.

modern, systematic theology, and his belief in "constant assiduous questioning" and debate brought him into conflict with the mystic Bernard of Clairvaux, who believed in the certainties conferred by individual religious ecstasy. Although Bernard triumphed in their lifetime, and had Abelard excommunicated, it was Abelard's less dangerous, more predictable and easily controlled approach that increasingly became adopted by the Church authorities.

depths, and he was far deeper." Bernard also warned that the spiritual union of the bride and bridegroom should not be interpreted physically. In both of these areas he differs from St Mechthild of Magdeburg (AD1207–97), who perceived the Sacrament as receiving "God's body" in the bread, after which "the godhead unites with our blameless soul and God's Manhood mingles with our flesh". Mechthild described God as waiting for her on the couch of his innermost chambers, and telling her, "You must cast off these two things: fear and shame, as well as all exterior virtues. It is only those that you carry within you by nature that you must desire to feel eternally: these virtues are your noble desire and your insatiable hunger which I shall satisfy eternally."

One of the last of the great love mystics, the 16th-century Spaniard St Teresa of Ávila, described her experiences of union with the divine in the same passionate terms as Mechthild. Teresa, however, appeared to be more aware of the fine distinction between spiritual ecstasy and "gluttony of the soul". This did not not prevent her from abandoning her lifelong friend and fellow love mystic, John of the Cross, after he warned her that her visions might not all be coming from God. When Teresa became mother of an abbey, she

Giovanni Bernini's Ecstasy of St Teresa *(1647–52) evokes the utter transport of Teresa's experience and her surrender to her vision.*

frequently reprimanded followers whose own experiences seem to have been little different from her own. One lay sister was told that she was not wanted for her raptures, but for washing dishes.

HILDEGARD OF BINGEN

St Hildegard of Bingen (1098–1179), in contrast to the other love mystics, sometimes depicted God's love as being feminine, or even maternal. Known as the prophetess of the Rhine, owing to her many revelations, she developed an elaborate theology in which the universe in all its workings corresponded to the human body, because: "Man, too, is God's handiwork [and] also God's journeyman, and the foreshadowing of the mysteries of God." Hildegard compared the Trinity itself to what she saw as the three components of sexual intercourse: strength, desire and action.

Eve and Mary

Their attitude toward women forced the early Christian thinkers to establish the absolute purity of the mother of Christ. Because Eve had tempted Adam in the Garden of Eden, women were seen as the vessels of sin, which was transmitted to their wombs at conception. The pains of childbirth and menstruation were the curses of Eve, and, according to Augustine, in the "faeces and urine" of childbirth men could see the closeness of women to all that was vile and corruptible. By contrast, Mary, who had not conceived or given birth like other women, was a second Eve, come to redeem the mistakes of the first. Eve was the fleshly mother of humanity, Mary its mother in spirit.

As such, she quickly became an object of worship in her own right. The first recorded prayer to the Virgin dates from c.AD390; her cult probably reached its peak between the millennium and the mid-16th century. The troubadours (see pp.84–5), encouraged by the Church, began to address their love poems to Mary rather than to an earthly mistress. The Ave Maria (Hail Mary) was added to the Lord's Prayer in the 11th century, and became an Office of the Church in the 12th, when the common title, Our Lady, also came into general use.

In popular worship, however, Mary may lose her virginal status. She has often been given the properties of the pagan mother goddesses who preceded her. The first recorded homage to her (described by St Epiphanius in the 4th century) is by Arab women offering cakes and wine in the hope of fertility, at a shrine where they used to worship Ashtaroth, queen of heaven. In Catholic countries, she still recalls the queen of the May (from Maia, a Greek nymph and fertility goddess) when her statue is carried through the streets, crowned and decked with flowers. In the 14th century, Mary protected adulterous women from

Mary squeezing milk from her breast onto the wounds of a sufferer, from the 14th-century English Queen Mary Psalter. *Lactation was the only normal biological function of motherhood that the Virgin was generally allowed to display, and from the 12th or 13th century, stories circulated of Mary expressing her milk onto sores to bring about a miraculous healing. These stories led to a vast 13th-century traffic in phials of preserved milk, and pieces of rock from the Milk Grotto in Bethlehem, where Mary is supposed to have nursed Jesus.*

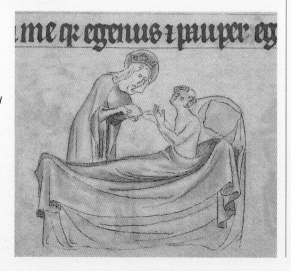

Pagan mother figures survived into Christianity in many guises, such as this Sheela-na-gig, on a 12th-century English church.

discovery by taking their place in the marriage bed, and she was often claimed in marriage herself, by votaries slipping a ring on to the finger of her statue. She could be murderously vengeful to an unfaithful husband.

However, Mary's most striking pagan metamorphosis occurs within orthodox doctrine, because she is identified with the Church, and the Church is the bride of Christ. Therefore, like Inanna of Sumer, and many other goddesses, Mary becomes the bride in an incestuous marriage with her own son.

As an ideal of perfection, the Virgin Mary has been used by the Church not to represent women, but to blame them by comparison. She is regarded as the patroness of priests and the guardian of their celibacy. Seminarians may still be urged to think of Mary if they have lustful thoughts, continuing a tradition, dating back to the troubadours, of sublimating desire in an unattainable fantasy figure.

MARY MAGDALENE

Christianity has often had an ambivalent attitude to prostitution. Pope Julius II, at the beginning of the 16th century, was said to have established a Church brothel in Rome, based on an earlier model at Avignon, where the inhabitants spent their time at religious duties when they were not servicing clients.

To the medieval Church, unmarried women were either virgins or whores, and the cult of Mary Magdalene grew alongside that of the Virgin Mary. As a prostitute who was redeemed, and became first an ascetic hermit and then a saint, the figure of the Magdalene neatly emphasized the Church's equation of women, fleshly temptation and sin, while at the same time holding out the promise of salvation to the penitent. The Magdalene of Western folklore is actually a conflation of at least three different biblical figures, who in the Orthodox Greek Church still have their feasts on separate days: Mary Magdalene herself, a woman from whom seven

Mary Magdalene (c.1456), a wood sculpture by Donatello. The ascetic Magdalene is sometimes shown naked, covered by her own hair.

demons were once exorcized by Jesus, and to whom he first appeared after his resurrection; Mary of Bethany, the sister of Lazarus, who bathes Christ's feet in ointment in the gospel of John; and an unspecified "sinner" – not explicitly a prostitute – who bathes Christ's feet or head in ointment in the other three gospels.

The image of the Magdalene also became confused with that of Mary of Egypt, who made a pilgrimage to the Holy Land in the 4th century by working her passage as a ship's prostitute. In Jerusalem she repented and vowed to become a hermit: she lived in the desert for forty-seven years. Many similar figures entered the canon as, in the words of the art historian Emil Mâle (1878–1954), "beauty consuming itself like incense burned before God in solitude far from the eyes of men became the most stirring image of penance conceivable".

Confession

Although confession is not a uniquely Christian phenomenon, it has been argued that only Christianity has a tradition of private confession to an official priesthood which has the power to forgive and absolve. The term generally refers to the confession of sins, although St Augustine (AD354–430) distinguished between confessions (or declarations) of faith, praise and sin. Even by his time, however, "there are some of the faithful who are so little informed that, when they hear the scripture speaking of confession, they immediately beat their breasts as if there could be no confession other than of sins". In the New Testament, James recommends that anyone who is ill should "confess your sins to one another, and pray for one another, and you shall be healed". To the early Christians, physical health and spiritual salvation were analogous. Augustine said, "Admit the healing hand, make your confession", and the penitential of St Columbanus spoke of the spiritual Doctors of the Church, who, like "doctors of the body" were able to provide "diverse kinds of cures for the wounds of the soul".

In the early Church, confession was a public act, made only once in a person's lifetime. By the 8th century, Christians had to confess their more serious sins regularly, and in AD760, the bishop Chrodegang of Metz ordered members of the Church to confess twice a year, at

The Confession *by Pietro Longhi (1702–88). Although meant to shield women from lustful priests, the confession box itself often hid seduction attempts.*

Lent and in the autumn. A later Rule of Chrodegang specified that monks should confess every Saturday. Until the Lateran Council of 1215, a layperson could hear the confession of another layperson, although without the power of absolution. The Council made it compulsory to confess to a priest.

From about the 10th century, confessors were required to take up an inquisitorial role, and ask detailed questions about every sexual variant or misdeed mentioned in their penitentials (books containing rules relating to penance), from bestiality to involuntary nocturnal emissions. The confessional quickly became open to abuse, and priests often refused to absolve certain women except for payment in the form of sexual favours. The ecclesiastical authorities were extremely lenient toward such priests at a time when other sexual offences were heavily punished: one Valdemar, tried in Toledo in 1535 for seducing two women and refusing absolution to another unless she slept with him, was fined two ducats and sentenced to thirty days seclusion in church before he was allowed to take his next confession. It was partly to hide women from lascivious clergymen that the Catholic Church prescribed the confessional box for all churches in 1614.

SPIRIT HEALERS

In many cultures, spirit healers sometimes become possessed so that they can interrogate the evil spirits in and around a patient, which are held to cause psychological symptoms such as hysteria and nervous attacks. In this way they are assuming the authority of the spirit realm in order to effect a cure by inducing a process of confession and penance. This authority resembles that of a priest, or indeed of a psychotherapist – the procedure is often similar to forms of Western therapy. In Puerto Rico, *espiritistas* (spiritual consultants) may progress from surface causes ("you are plagued by spirits sent against you by jealous colleagues") to underlying vulnerabilities (patients admitting they are having marital difficulties, making them susceptible to attack).

CONFESSION AND TRUTH

The French philosopher and historian Michel Foucault (1926–84) believed that the last 300 years have seen a "discursive explosion" surrounding sex. While the apparent repression of sexuality became more pronounced, the actual discussion of all elements of sexuality became increasingly pervasive. In the confessional, the individual was required to confess in ever greater detail his or her desires, thoughts and acts. Desire, processed through the "endless mill of speech", was transformed into knowledge, or truth.

Foucault contrasts Western culture with other, especially Eastern, cultures, that have had an *ars erotica* (a body of sexual lore), via which "sex served as a medium for initiations into learning": that is, truth was derived from sex. Western society has evolved a *scientia sexualis*, in which confession is the medium for producing truth, and "it is in the confession that truth and sex are joined, through the obligatory and exhaustive expression of an individual secret". Confession is compulsive and mandatory, having spread far beyond the Christian confessional, into

legal, medical and, especially, psychiatric and psychoanalytic practices. Foucault argues that the spread of confessional techniques produces an understanding of the self as possessing a truth, which demands to be known. This understanding of the subject (or self) promotes ever more and refined confessional techniques and calls forth a variety of secular priests, or experts, to interpret the confession.

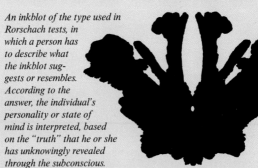

An inkblot of the type used in Rorschach tests, in which a person has to describe what the inkblot suggests or resembles. According to the answer, the individual's personality or state of mind is interpreted, based on the "truth" that he or she has unknowingly revealed through the subconscious.

Witches

The first witches mentioned by Christian writers were groups, mostly of women, who gathered to worship pre-Christian mother goddesses and horned fertility gods. The early medieval Church, anxious to establish Christianity as the one true religion, was more concerned to combat belief in the effectiveness of witchcraft than to persecute witches themselves. As a result, it was lenient, and at times even protective, toward people who were accused of practising witchcraft. The Synod of Paderborn in AD785 ordered the death penalty for anyone who put a person to death for being a witch, a ruling later confirmed by Emperor Charlemagne (AD742–814).

An engraving from Guazzo's Compendium Maleficarum (1608) of a woman kissing the Devil's behind. The "obscene kiss" was one of the accepted criteria of heresy, but the confessions of several witches indicated that in their ceremonies they were actually kissing a mask, fixed to the rear of an officiating pagan priest.

The attitude of the Church began to change in the 14th century, with Pope John XXII. In the late 15th century, under Innocent VIII, it became a heresy to deny the reality of witchcraft. John's first papal bull against witchcraft emphasized the power of witches to do harm, but by the time Innocent issued his bull *Summa desiderantes*, the emphasis was on sex, lust, temptation and the power of witches to cause impotence and infertility: "They hinder men from performing the sexual act, and women from conceiving, whence husbands cannot know their wives, nor wives receive their husbands."

Innocent had drawn up the bull at the request of Heinrich Kramer and James Sprenger, Dominican inquisitors whose fanaticism had already alienated local bishops and clergy. In 1486, Sprenger and Kramer published the hugely influential and popular *Malleus Maleficarum* (Hammer of Witches), which went through ten editions in only a few years. The use of the feminine form,

The Witches' Sabbath *(c.1821), by Goya. The Devil, often called "God's Ape", provides a mirror image of the deity, with his Masses, churches, disciples and rites parodying those of Christianity.*

maleficarum (literally, wrongdoers), is significant: the text specifies that women are more prone to witchcraft than men, primarily because "all witchcraft comes from carnal lust, which in women is insatiable". Consequently, women were the main victims of witch-hunts. King James I of England, in his *Daemonologie* of 1597, thought that twenty women were executed to every one man, but other contemporary estimates put the ratio at between fifty and 100 to one.

In 1585, two villages in the Bishopric of Trier in Germany were left with only one surviving female each. A bishop of Geneva burned 500 witches in three months, and 800 people were condemned at one trial by the Senate of Savoy. It has been claimed that, until 1914, more people in Europe were killed in witch-hunts than in war. In North America, belief in witchcraft was prevalent in Puritan communities, and more than thirty people were condemned in the infamous witch-trials held at Salem, Massachusetts, in 1692.

However, the tradition of witchcraft was never entirely wiped out, and the 20th century has seen the emergence of the Wicca movement (see pp.156–9).

DEMON LOVERS

A succubus was a demon who was thought to assume the shape of a woman in order to seduce a man and to use his seed for the propagation of more demons. An alternative theory was that, having slept with a man as a succubus, the demon transformed itself into a male, or incubus, and seduced a woman, passing on the seed it had acquired in its female form. Reginald Scot, in his *Discoverie of Witchcraft* (1584), described the incubus as a fantasy occurring to women with "melancholie abounding in their heads" – although some incubus manifestations had a more concrete explanation. One incubus appeared to a woman and made such "hot loove unto hir" that she screamed, and when the household entered her room they found the demon hiding under her bed, as Scot drily remarks, in the likeness of one Bishop Sylvanus.

Accusations of witchcraft always included the charge that the witch had allowed the Devil to perform acts of sodomy, despite the freezing coldness of his member. Witches were also accused of performing orgies at their black sabbaths, and of having intercourse with their familiars: demons in the form of animals such as cats, frogs or crows.

An engraving depicting a succubus. The demons serving the Devil were arranged in hierarchies and legions, in mockery of the hosts of heaven: incubi and succubi were the lowest form of demon.

The rediscovery of the body

The Renaissance of the 15th and 16th centuries revived Greek art and culture in the West, and used the principles derived from them as a vehicle to glorify the individual. The Renaissance had its beginnings in the Humanist ideas propagated by the 14th-century Italian poet and scholar Petrarch. Humanism, building on the beliefs of the ancient Greeks, placed humankind, not God, at the centre of the universe and emphasized the unity of human beings and nature. While it set a high value on individualism and the full development of human potential, Renaissance Humanism was not a secular movement, and its ideas ran in parallel with rather than in opposition to Christian teachings.

The "Tauride Venus" (3rd century BC), a Roman copy of a Greek statue: an idealized classical image of beauty.

Influential classical works included sculptures such as the *Belvedere Torso* and *Apollo Belvedere*, the literature of Plato and Pliny the Elder, and Marcus Vitruvius's book *De Architectura*. Following classical ideals, Renaissance artists became increasingly interested in the human body. Medieval cosmologies had seen it as a microcosm of the universe, controlled by the movements of the stars and planets; the naked body was viewed with a kind of revulsion, and when portrayed in art it had been as the outward expression of souls in torment – starved, pathetic and suffering. With the advent of the Renaissance, the body became the measure of the universe, and housed a free, noble spirit. For the first time since the Greeks, it was regularly depicted naked – not to show loss, poverty or suffering, but as an object of beauty and power, finely muscled and strong, in dignified, self-assured poses.

The influence of Plato on Renaissance thinking was profound. In Neoplatonism, his emphasis on the spiritual was used to link classical philosophy with Christian thought. A slightly different effect was generated by the Renaissance reading of the *Symposium* – Plato's frankest description of the nature of love – which inspired a partial revival of the noble pederastic ideal (see pp. 46–7) – although there is some evidence that the ideal was not reflected in actual behaviour.

The men and women of the Renaissance conceived of beauty itself as an overriding form of virtue. This, too, was an attitude that they took from the Greeks, who saw in a beautiful form the mark of the deity. (In ancient Greece, when the courtesan Phryne was taken to court, she bared her breasts and was acquitted. The judges were not, apparently, acting out of desire, but because, in the words of the 2nd-century BC Greek writer Athenaus, "they were seized with holy awe of the divinity".)

This equation of the holy with the

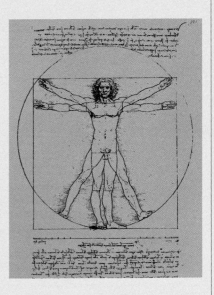

Vitruvian Man *(c.1490) by Leonardo da Vinci.*
The Renaissance adopted and expanded on the
classical idea that human beauty, like the
workings of the universe, was governed by
mathematical rules of proportion and harmony.

beautiful is one of the lasting legacies of
the Renaissance. Images of beauty have
commonly been used to promote ideas,
such as the vision of an afterlife. In pre-
Renaissance Christian Europe, beauty
was ascribed to spirituality, and thus
associated with a state of being to which
the observer was intended to aspire. In
the Renaissance this equation was in-
verted, so that spirituality was imputed
to beauty, and beauty itself seen as a
state of virtue or holiness. In reviving
the Greek idealization of the body, the
Renaissance began the tradition of promoting beauty as the legitimate goal (or
possession) of a human life: a vision
that has been taken to an extreme in
present-day advertising. Beauty has
been transformed from a *sign* of transcendence to a *state* of
transcendence – a fantasy
that can be attained by the
proper exercise of wealth.

Partly as a reaction to
the strict conventions of
classical form, and partly
in reflection of the sexual
tastes of many of its leading artists and writers, the

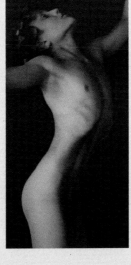

Male Nude *(1921), a*
photograph by František
Drtikol. The use of ambiguous,
androgynous figures to suggest
an other-worldly, mysterious
beauty is a trend that, from the
Renaissance, has survived into
the artistic vocabulary of the
20th century.

Renaissance was also fascinated with
physical ambiguity. The artists of the
time created a model of androgynous
beauty, through sculptures such as
Donatello's *David* and
paintings by, for example,
Verrocchio, Botticelli and
Leonardo. To many eyes,
androgyny may appear
non-naturalistic or artificial – a form that has been
deliberately sought or
manipulated. This makes
it (like its opposite, the
body-builder's profile)
appropriate as an icon of
a beauty that, far from
being innate, might be
attained. It is no coincidence that androgynes and
body-builders have been
recurrent images in 20th-
century advertising.

Protestantism: Puritans and love cults

The 16th-century Reformation of the Western Church attacked the principles of clerical celibacy and monastic vows of continence, although according to Max Weber in *The Protestant Ethic and the Spirit of Capitalism* (1904), this drove asceticism out of the cloister into the world, helping to create the repressive climate of the Puritans. But Protestantism, like Catholicism, has endured extremes of behaviour: Puritanism was at least in part a reaction to the Anabaptists, who encouraged polygamy.

John Calvin (1509–64), the Genevan religious reformer, praised copulation as both honourable and holy. He attacked St Jerome (see pp.82–3) for damning sex as unclean, when scripture presented it as a symbol of the union between Christ and the Church. Another great Protestant reformer, Martin Luther (1483–1546), clung to the Pauline view of marriage as "a hospital for the sick": a partial cure for the incontinence plaguing men. For Luther, as for the early Church Fathers, sex held a stigma of shame deriving from the fall of Adam and Eve. But he advised anyone who was to be ordained not to swear continence: celibacy was possible only for "pecu-

liar" men: attempts to lead an ascetic life would almost inevitably lead to concubinage, a greater sin than marriage.

The Reformation retained the division of the human being into flesh and spirit (the flesh subordinate to and tending to corrupt the spirit). According to the Anglican Book of Common Prayer (1662), marriage was for the procreation of children and "a remedy against sin", yet until 1928 the baptism service stated

Portrait of three generations of a family *by Dirck Santvoort (1610–80).*

that "all men are conceived and born in sin". Until 1975, a Methodist prayer for baptized babies was that "all things belonging to the flesh may die in them".

Protestant theologians tended to ignore acts, such as sodomy, that had been branded "unnatural" by their Catholic predecessors. However, the 17th-century bishop Jeremy Taylor declared "sins against nature" to be no worse than other sins, such as adultery.

Taylor's notably modern insight was that sin arises because "men make necessities of their own [desires], and then find ways to satisfy them". His writings are among the earliest consistent Reformation attempts to reconcile sex and spirituality. In contrast to St Paul, he held that "single life makes men in one instance to be like angels, but marriage in very many things makes the chaste pair to be like Christ".

NEW UTOPIAS

The leaders of charismatic, non-conformist religious sects often create communities that they claim are based on the principle of *agape* (see p.75). The approach of such communities to sex varies from the complete abstinence of the North American Shakers (so successful that the movement has all but died out) to the sex-as-sacrament attitude of the Oneida Community, who practised "complex marriage", and whose children were sexually initiated at puberty by older community members. A group's approach to sex, as determined by its leader, frequently becomes the main instrument of leadership. To control a person's sexuality provides a sense that one's power extends beyond the outer, social world, into the inner, psychological and spiritual realm. This sense of control may fuel an already Messianic temperament, with terrible results, as in 1993 when David Koresh's community at Waco, Texas, was destroyed following a siege.

Erotica and pornography

Indian temple carvings of the gods and goddesses in amorous play (see p.146), like the explicit scrolls given as Japanese bridal trousseaus (see p.134), were meant to uplift, educate and amuse observers as much as to arouse them. The perceived dividing line between pornography and this sort of erotica varies from individual to individual, and is conditioned by religious beliefs, upbringing, personal experience and received opinion as to what constitutes art and culture. For this reason, a society's approach to, and definition of, pornography is an excellent barometer of the zeitgeist, or spirit of the time.

For example, the publication in 1948 and 1953 of Alfred Kinsey's massive sociological reports on sexual behaviour in the United States sparked an increasing openness about sex, leading to the "sexual revolution" of the 1960s and early 1970s. During this period, among other notable events, Betty Friedan published *The Feminine Mystique* (1963), generally considered the beginning of the women's liberation movement; in 1965 the US Supreme Court

Salomé: the stomach dance, *by Aubrey Beardsley, from a series of illustrations to Oscar Wilde's* Salomé *(1894). The explicit nature of both the drawings and the play caused a scandal.*

legalized the sale of contraceptives throughout the United States; and in 1969 Denmark became the first Western country to drop all laws against the publication or sale of pornography. At the time, pornography was seen by many liberal thinkers as a vehicle of free speech and a weapon against authority.

The critic Susan Sontag, writing in 1967, compared the pornographic and religious imaginations, as two all-inclusive ways of describing the world. For Sontag, the pornographic universe "is a total universe. It has the power to ingest and metamorphose and translate all concerns that are fed into it", and turn them into the "one negotiable currency" that is the need for erotic exchange – just as religion turns them

Popular Japanese Shunga (erotic) prints such as this 18th-century example were based on classical Chinese art.

work was merely a pretext. Even the medieval Catholic Church, with its numerous laws against sex, confined its censorship of the written word to instances of heresy or political subversion. Boccaccio's *Decameron* (*c*.1350) was stripped of heretical passages but allowed into circulation with its erotic content intact.

The growth of mass-printing techniques in the 15th century, and the development of a large public eager for ever more sensational entertainment, led to censorship purely on grounds of obscenity. The British Crown, like many ruling bodies, was fearful of anything that might excite the "unformed minds" and "brute passions" of the masses. The first ever obscenity ruling was in England in 1727, against Edmund Curll, publisher of *Venus of the Cloister: or, the Nun in her Smock*, when Mr Justice Probyn made the far-reaching declaration that "morality is part of the law of the land as Christianity is" and any act "destructive of morality in general" should be punished in the same way as blasphemy. The 18th-century law-makers, like their successors, put some faith in the power of education to preserve morals. Classically inspired poems and paintings might deal with forbidden subjects; and in the early 20th century, film-makers such as D.W. Griffith used a high moral tone and classical subjects to render nudity acceptable on the carefully policed cinema screens.

CENSORSHIP AND THE CLASSICS

The earliest recorded example of censorship, in 411BC, was the banning of Aristophanes' play *Lysistrata*, about women who withhold sex from their husbands to force them to stop fighting a war. Although extremely bawdy, the play was outlawed solely for its satire on the state of Athens. Similarly, in AD7, when the Roman Emperor Augustus banished Ovid for writing the *Ars Amatoria* (Art of Love), his motives were political, and the obscenity of the

---

all into the hunger for God. This is why pornographers such as the Marquis de Sade (see p.116–19), Georges Bataille and the pseudonymous Pauline Réage (author of *The Story of O*) allow no sexual taboos and make no distinction between the sexes, or between humans and animals or humans and objects. They are multiplying the possibilities of exchange. Bataille especially is clear that eroticism – like poetry, violence and religious sacrifice – leads to "the blending and fusion of separate objects. It leads us to eternity, it leads us to death, and through death to continuity."

Not all pornography has so profound an effect: it is often merely a vehicle for fantasy and escape. Nevertheless, the most extreme forms of modern Western pornography are, in Sontag's analysis, among the "demonic vocabularies" that answer the human need for personal transcendence since religion has begun to fail in that role.

The unfamiliar

Conquerors have always used the sexual customs of the vanquished as an excuse to label them barbarians and incidentally justify their own oppressions. Even Genghis Khan, upon conquering one Chinese province, claimed to be so horrified that the local Buddhist priest deflowered virgin girls that he had the man ritually dismembered (thus removing a potential source of opposition). This tendency reached its nadir between the 16th and 19th centuries, in wave after wave of European colonial expansion followed by campaigns to convert the heathens and save them from the consequences of their ignorance and sin. Sexual customs acted as a powerful rationale for such exploitation. At one time, so many Spanish atrocities in the Americas were justified as attempts to wipe out the endemic sin of sodomy that the theologian Francisco de Vitoria wondered why France did not use that excuse to conquer Italy.

While some colonial powers subjugated peoples in the course of "saving" them, others tried to show that there was nothing to save: that these were soulless brutes, having no rights that needed to be worried about. Such attempts to dehumanize other peoples concentrated to a great extent on notions of physical beauty, and on trivial differences in secondary sexual characteristics. In the 18th century, the beard became a popular device for differentiating between peoples,

The Nama or Khoikhoi (Hottentots) of southern Africa typically have a lot of fat on the buttocks (steatopygia). In the 18th century, the "Hottentot Venus" was celebrated in Europe for her beauty; however, when she died her body was dissected in an attempt scientifically to classify her "otherness".

as it had long been a way of differentiating between the sexes. The absence of beards in women confirmed their lack of nobility: they did not have this "sign of majesty" because they were born subject to men (Hatshepsut, the only queen apart from Cleopatra to rule Egypt single-handedly, was often given a beard on her statues). The lack of a beard in Native American males was taken as proof of their similar subjection. One group of Americans was

America (c.1600), an engraving by Jan van der Straet. The New World is allegorized as a woman, naked and vulnerable before the conqueror, Amerigo Vespucci. The metaphor emphasizes how new lands were seen as virgin territory to be plundered by male explorers from "civilized" Europe.

SEXUAL HYPOCRISY

Western colonizers were often attracted by the people and practices they claimed to despise. Late 19th-century Anglican missionaries in Papua New Guinea complained of native immorality, but the Papuans maintained that the worst morals were found in the mission houses. One bishop of North Queensland extolled the delights of Papuan youths, who, he claimed, combined the character of St John with the physique of Apollo. In Africa it was not unusual for men who preached chastity to father children by native women; the Wesleyan Rev. Bernasko, in Dahomey (Benin), had so many daughters that in 1874 he turned his mission into a brothel in which to prostitute them.

The ambivalence of the colonial attitude is also evident in descriptions of Indian temple prostitution (see pp.26–9). Abbé Dubois, in the 18th century, condemned temple rituals – "A religion more shameful or indecent has never existed among a civilized people" – but he also described the "elegant and attractive attire", "beautiful hair", "infinite taste" and "graceful carriage" of these "enchanting sirens".

Colonial ambivalence was often reflected in the attitudes of local people: this uncondemning 18th-century painting of a white man and an Indian woman copulating is by an Indian artist.

enslaved by the Spanish ostensibly because they ate unpalatable food, smoked tobacco and "trimmed their scanty beards in an unseemly fashion".

At the same time, Western scientists were attempting to classify women according to their breasts (see pp.102–3). Those of African women were depicted as sagging, hanging like "great sacks to the waist", and stories abounded of women flinging them over their shoulders to feed the babies that they carried on their backs. The ideal Enlightenment breast was firm and spherical; sagging breasts represented hags, witches and fallen women. So African women, like European witches, were equated with chaotic nature and untrammelled sexuality, an equation

used to justify buying and selling them into prostitution and concubinage.

Aesthetics had a major influence on theories of race in the 18th and 19th centuries. The naturalist Johann Blumenbach (1752–1840) invented the term Caucasian for the white or light-skinned division of humankind. He believed that the Caucasus region of Europe was the birthplace of humankind, partly because it contained light-skinned people, and pale skin can darken but, he thought, dark skin never lightens: from this, he reasoned that all races were degenerations from this extreme of paleness. But his main reason for choosing this site was because it contained Georgia, and for Blumenbach, Georgian women were the most beautiful on earth.

Sex and science

Ever since the civilization of ancient Babylon, chaotic nature has been represented as female: fruitful and creative but needing to be dissected, shaped and controlled by male reason (see pp.32–3). In the 17th century, the English philosopher Francis Bacon, credited with being the inspiration behind the Royal Society (Britain's oldest scientific society, founded in 1660) and the inventor of inductive reasoning, described a marriage between mind and nature, promising to lead his reader to "nature and all her children to bind her to your service and make her your slave". Bacon was writing against a background of the widespread persecution of witches (see pp.92–3), and his descriptions of the scientific process include images of nature as a female, to be restrained, tortured and probed by mechanical inventions: "Neither ought a man to make scruple of entering and penetrating into these holes and corners, when the inquisition of truth is his whole object …"

Sexual difference itself became an overwhelming preoccupation of science during the Enlightenment of the 18th century, with a systematic exploration of the differences between the sexes, based on anatomy. Older or more traditional cultures had used ritual to link the social and natural worlds, so that the former assumed the authority of the latter (see pp.36–9), and in a similar way, the rationalist thinkers of the Enlightenment claimed that nature prescribed the social laws that they wished to follow. In 1735, the Swedish botanist Linnaeus published his classification of plants, describing them in terms of their sexual parts; the male were the dominant, defining parts, the female were secondary and submissive. Examples such as this were used as natural (that is, biological) legitimation for the idea that men and women were not equals, but complementary opposites.

By such means, the identification of women with nature and emotion, men with culture and reason was retained.

The physician Erasmus Darwin (1731–1802; grandfather of the naturalist Charles Darwin) was one of the most fervent popularizers of the Linnaean system of plant classification. His book The Loves of the Plants *(1791) contains lurid descriptions – in the form of heroic poetry – of the sexual reproduction of plants. One flower, "in her wane beauty" and "with fatal smiles" is described as seducing her own son; another bows with "wanton air", rolls her dark eyes and gratifies five different suitors. Darwin uses scientific theories and the "natural" behaviour of plants to expound the free love that he practised after the death of his first wife.*

Scientific grounds were used to "prove" that wet-nursing was a moral evil. This 18th-century engraving shows the wet-nurse to the child of Gabrielle d'Estrées, mistress of Henri IV.

own child. This accorded with the general approbation of the breast by the scientific and medical community of the time. The breast was a symbol of the natural bond between mother and child, and as such placed women firmly in the home at the centre of the family. It was therefore seen as biologically and morally good: and the advocation of breast-feeding was another way of extolling women's domestic roles and distancing them from the public domain.

The association of women with nature defined them as motherly and physical – so that their ideal environment was in the home as nurturers – but it was also used to link them to superstition, making them an impediment to progress. Both men and women were characterized by their biological makeup, but while the sphere in which men could act remained broad, external and unlimited, women's sphere of movement was tightly circumscribed by their "natural" function. In 1758, Linnaeus coined the term Mammalia, naming an entire class of animals after a feature (lactating mammary glands) that only half – the females – ever possess. Linnaeus could have chosen external body hair, for example, as a better defining characteristic. However, he was engaged in a propaganda war against wet-nursing, and was concerned to emphasize how natural it was for a mother to suckle her

TRUTH AND LOVE

The Greek philosopher Plato (*c.*429–*c.*347BC) was the first Western thinker to describe the acquisition of knowledge in erotic terms. Plato believed that the human mind was a part of nature and that nature was permeated with mind: but that nature was also trapped in disorder, just as the human mind was trapped in its body. Plato located truth in a world of perfect, unchanging forms that lay behind and above the visible, transient world: knowledge was attained when the mind learned to escape the claims of the senses, and become one with these images of perfection. In the *Republic*, he describes the task of the philosopher as being to grasp the essential nature of things by using the faculty in the mind "which is akin to reality, and which approaches and unites with it": *unites* in the original being *syneimi*, denoting sexual intercourse. In the *Symposium*, he explains how the mind frees itself from the distractions of the mortal body: using the power of Eros (here, non-physical love), the souls of two lovers contemplate and mirror each other, projecting each other ever closer to truth.

Symbols, Symptoms and Taboos

The sex drive is irresistible, if not for every individual at all times, then for the species as a whole. It has to be, in order for the species to survive. Such an overpowering instinct often has to be denied by the rational mind, or transformed – sublimated into some other activity, such as art or religion, or expressed only through a confusing and contradictory code of symbols and obsessions.

Sometimes these patterns of displaced images and activities are intensely personal, as with the fetishist's particular object of desire; and an individual's failure to indulge his or her compulsion can cause anguish or misery. Often, such expressions of sublimated sexuality are common to an entire people, and become the focus of social ritual – such as initiation ceremonies. In this case, the failure to perform them correctly can be held to blame for a whole range of personal and natural disasters.

The Garden of Earthly Delights *(centre panel) by Hieronymus Bosch* (c.1450–1516). *It has been claimed that Bosch's perversely erotic icons were subversive, or even heretical in nature. They are more likely to have been highly personal moral fables, revealing the artist's own sex-related phobias, nightmares and dreams. Nonetheless, the painting borrows from the widespread medieval tradition of depicting nude bodies in states of* extremis, *as a warning against sexual temptation.*

Sigmund Freud

Sigmund Freud (1856–1939) described himself as one of a trinity of revolutionary scientific thinkers who progressively removed the godlike pretensions of humankind: first Copernicus (1473–1543) proved that humanity was not at the centre of the universe; then Darwin (1809–82) showed that humanity was not created in God's image but was descended from ape-like creatures; and finally Freud, with his

A photograph of Freud taken in 1921.

exposition of the unconscious mind, demonstrated that only a fraction of human thought is rational. Further, in *Totem and Taboo* (1913), he traced the whole genesis of art, religion and culture back to a sublimation, or redirection, of sexual motives and the guilt arising from them.

In the unconscious, Freud located the pleasure principle, a set of desires and impulses driven by the instincts and mostly sexual in nature. Because these desires are disorganized and often dangerous or destructive, they have to be controlled by the rational, far-sighted reality principle of the conscious mind. The unconscious also contains a repressing mechanism, which can bury the memory of traumatic incidents with the result that, unlike ordinary memories, they cannot dissipate over time. Instead, they remain as a powerful,

repetitive motivating force on an individual's behaviour, which can give rise to hysterical symptoms such as paralysis or hallucinations. Psychoanalysis is the process of uncovering these memories and their attendant emotions, so that they can be experienced and forgotten normally.

According to Freud, everyone is born with a libido or sex drive that is polymorphously perverse, or capable of taking sexual pleasure in the stimulation of any part of the body. The sex drive has no "natural" object: the complex structure of an adult's libido is determined in several

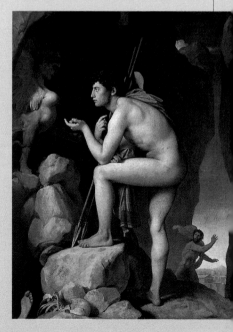

Oedipus and the Sphinx, *by J.A.D. Ingres (1780–1867). The myth of Oedipus, who unwittingly killed his father and married his mother, provided Freud with his central metaphor for the development of the infant psyche.*

stages during infancy, during any one of which things can go wrong and traumas or perversions arise. The oral stage is characterized by the baby's pleasure in suckling, and sense of loss when the breast is withdrawn. The anal stage is when the child associates pleasure (and creativity) with the conscious control of its bowels, before it enters the phallic stage and discovers genital masturbation. At this stage both boys and girls are supposed to feel they have phallic procreative powers, and believe they can give their mothers a child, or even produce one from their own anuses. This leads at the age of five or six to the Oedipus complex, when the desire for an incestuous relationship with the mother creates a fear of (and a repressed wish to kill) the father. Boys develop a fear of being castrated by their vengeful fathers; girls discover they are already castrated,

develop penis envy and may resent their mothers for bringing them into the world incomplete. Most of Freud's theories were controversial when he coined them, and some have become more controversial since, but his influence on Western thought is incalculable.

THE EGO AND THE ID

Freud recognized that not all unconscious drives could be sexual. In 1920 he proposed the existence of the death instinct, or Thanatos: a nostalgia on the part of all living matter for a state of inorganic inertia. It was balanced by Eros, the reproductive life instinct that ensures the survival of the species. In 1923 Freud proposed a new model of the mind, comprising the id, which contains the primitive, instinctual urges; the ego, which engages with reality and unconsciously represses the id; and the superego, the "conscience" or image of parental authority, which gradually takes the place of repressed Oedipal urges.

THE DREAMING FATHER

An apostolic succession of psychoanalysts descends from Freud, all of whom are themselves analyzed before they can practise. Uniquely, as the father of psychoanalysis, Freud analyzed himself, drawing to a great extent on the interpretation of his own dreams. This self-analysis is itself often presented by Freudians in mythic terms: as an heroic and dangerous journey into the underworld of the mind to bring back some secret wisdom.

Freud believed that all dreams represented the fulfilment of unconscious, usually sexual, wishes. But the sexual wish can only appear in a disguised form, which is the origin of dream symbols. Although dreaming is perfectly

normal, Freud thought that it gave an insight into the disordered mind, because the displacement of the real content of a dream on to some apparently unrelated object is similar to the process that occurs in obsessional neuroses.

Freud dreamed of his mother being carried by a bird-headed Egyptian god (such as Thoth, shown here on a papyrus dating from c.1250BC), which he interpreted as a sexual wish, because the German slang for sex, vögeln, *also means birds.*

Carl Jung

Carl Gustav Jung (1875–1961) was the only son of a Swiss Reformed Church evangelical minister, and was obsessed by religion from early childhood. He used to fantasize that God forced him to think abominable thoughts as a condition for the bestowal of grace. Jung dated his own intellectual life from a dream at the age of three, in which he descended into the ground and saw a phallic object sitting on a golden throne. In the

A photograph of Jung dating from the 1930s.

dream his mother told him, "That's the man-eater", and he awoke in terror. Jung, who often played in churches and graveyards, came to associate this enthroned phallus with the Jesus he heard invoked each time that bodies were put into the ground. Both were aspects of the dark force of creation that he pursued for the rest of his life.

Jung first became interested in psychiatry because of his fascination with spiritualism and the nature of the soul. He described psychiatry as "a place where the collision of nature and spirit became a reality". In 1906 he met Freud, with whom he struck up a rapport, becoming the "crown prince of the psychoanalytic movement". But already there were major differences between the two men. Freud's approach to the unconscious mind was non-spiritualist; Jung thought that Freud placed too much emphasis on sex. For Jung, the pleasure a child took at the mother's breast was only the normal satisfaction gained from eating, which Freud was confusing with a uniquely adult type of sexual instinct. Whereas Freud thought the incestuous Oedipal complex – the childhood fantasy of murdering the father and possessing the mother – was a literal (if unconscious) wish to penetrate the mother, Jung saw it as a desire for spiritual rebirth.

Jung became increasingly critical of the exclusively sexual basis of Freud's theories. He began to study astrology as well as parapsychology, at first careful to preserve his friendship with Freud by using the "correct" terminology. He promised to return from his "religious libidinal clouds" with "rich booty" for analysis. In 1912 he published *The Psychology of the Unconscious*, based on his independent researches, and by 1913, Freud was referring to "that brutal and sanctimonious Jung", and applied a classical Oedipal analysis to their relationship: the jealous Jung wished to kill "his father" Freud and possess psychoanalysis ("the beautiful mother") for himself.

After the split, Jung became more fascinated with the relationship between psychotic fantasies and ancient myths, and developed his theory of the collective unconscious: residual memories or archetypes that lie buried not just in the individual mind but in the minds of all humanity. Jung understood these archetypes as being self-portraits of the common human instincts. He believed that the psyche strives toward wholeness and equilibrium: to become a self.

ALCHEMICAL ARCHETYPES

According to Jung, empirical science had deadened the part of the imagination that dealt in myth, with the result that the Western world could no longer experience the mysterious. In the latter part of his life, the

An alchemical engraving from Michael Maier's Symbola Auraea *(1617). The hermaphrodite is a "chemical marriage" of male and female.*

scope of his researches became ever broader, encompassing, among other areas, the significance of dreams and drawings, and the symbolism of religions and myths.

Jung turned to medieval alchemy to provide a model for his own psychological theories, publishing *Psychology and Alchemy* in 1944. His work led to a revival of interest in this area of occult knowledge (see p.157). He emphasized the alchemist's search for the philosopher's stone, which would transmute base metals into gold, as a quest for spiritual transformation. In alchemy, the philosopher's stone resulted from the union of divine opposites, of dark and light, and for Jung was a symbol of the self. Analysis was itself the process of alchemy. Each of the alchemist's ingredients had a psychological equivalent, so that iron was brave and passionate, for example, while tin was honest and lofty. Mercury, the poisonous, deceptive, trans-formative element which made the union of opposites possible was, in Jung's formulation, the collective unconscious.

The self is composed of the conscious and the unconscious. Through dreams, images or pathological disease, the unconscious seeks to compensate for the attitudes of the conscious, to create a balance. Jung postulated four arche-typal figures working in pairs, one conscious and one unconscious, com-pensating for the conscious. The ego, the sense of purpose and identity, is bal-anced by the primitive, animal-like shadow. The persona, the mask a per-son presents to society, is balanced by the soul image. A man's soul image is female (the anima); a woman's is male (the animus). The soul image, although an archetype, can be modified by actual experiences of the opposite sex, espe-cially parents, but it can, equally, be projected onto members of the opposite sex, creating a distorted image of them.

Salome with the Head of John the Baptist, *by J. Vergeses. Salome was an archetypal "shadow".*

Wilhelm Reich

Wilhelm Reich (1897–1957) entered the Vienna University Medical School as a war veteran in 1918. Within a year he was attending unofficial student seminars in sexology, and he became convinced that sexuality was "the centre around which revolves the whole of social life as well as the inner life of the individual". In 1920 he became a member of the Vienna Psychoanalytic Society, which at that time was under the direction of Freud (see pp.106–7). The two men were friends, and Freud referred patients to Reich even though he had not undergone a full Freudian training. Gradually, however, Reich moved away from Freud, and began to evolve his own ideas about the relationship between mind and body.

In *The Function of Orgasm* (1927), Reich developed the idea that orgastic potency, or the potential to experience complete, uninhibited orgasm, was vital to the healthy adult; failure to release pent-up sexual energy in this way could result in deep-seated neuroses. But in general, Reich's early work was more concerned with overall character than with individual neurotic symptoms. In *Character Analysis* (1933) he proposed that a person's "character structure" could be used as a kind of armour to stop the individual discovering his or her own underlying neuroses. He also developed his idea of physiological anchoring: that a psychic experience may lead to the lasting physical alteration of an organ in the human body. By creating a framework of permanently tensed or paralyzed muscles, emotions could work to create a second kind of character armour, that was apparently purely physical. Reich

Reich was not the first to examine the various effects of orgasm. This print, showing an "electro-physiological analysis of the effects of the passions" was the result of work analyzing facial expressions and associated emotions, carried out in the 1850s by Dr G.B. Duchenne and Adrien Tournachon.

believed that it was possible to relieve mental problems directly by manipulation and massage of the body. This therapeutic technique – known as orgasm therapy, or vegetotherapy – supposedly destroys the muscular armouring of the body and liberates the vegetative (autonomic) nervous system to enable full and satisfying orgasm, which Reich had identified as the key to mental health.

During his early career, Reich had grown increasingly involved in sexual liberation movements, which ultimately led to his split from the psychoanalytic establishment in 1934. His ideas also became less orthodox. He claimed that he had measured a previously unknown energy discharge from the pelvis during orgasm. He named this orgone energy or orgone radiation (OR), declaring that it moved in spirals and was blue. It was the basic life-stuff – the cosmic energy that suffused and powered the nervous systems of all beings – and the answer to all religious and philosophical problems. When two orgone rays met they could form biones – intermediate building blocks between the inanimate and animate worlds – which could mass together to form protozoa.

Reich built orgone accumulation boxes to store this universal orgasmic energy. He sat patients in the boxes to cure them of colds, arthritis, anaemia and other disorders, including cancer. He also thought orgone energy might cure radiation sickness, and neutralize atom bombs. When he began distributing his orgone accumulators as cancer cures, he attracted the adverse attention of the US Food and Drug Authority. He died in prison, on a charge of contempt of court. Few would dispute that, at some point in his career, Reich's ideas became mad and worthless. But there is little agreement over exactly when.

THE HUNT FOR ORGONE

Reich's descriptions of orgone radiation are reminiscent of the ancient occult conception of the Astral Light, an all-pervading energy field or "ether of the wise". As a result, a number of Reichians have studied the occult, especially sex-magic (see pp.156–9). Many practising magicians have incorporated orgone into their rituals. The one-time secretary of the notorious occultist Aleister Crowley, Dr F.I. Regardie, became a Reichian analyst and vegetotherapist.

Orgone energy has been linked to the Kirlian aura (see right) – a corona around objects that can be photographed using high voltage, low-current electricity to expose the film. Reich claimed that orgone energy could be seen under microscopes and detected by geiger counters and thermometers, although it was completely different from electromagnetic energy, radioactivity or heat.

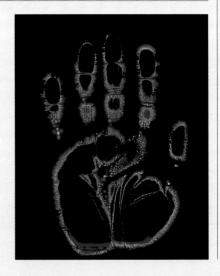

Types of love

Many creatures attract their mates with features or behaviour that seem to have no other evolutionary advantage. For example, the spectacular tails of peacocks make them more vulnerable to predators, but the larger (and more cumbersome) a peacock's tail, the more attractive it is to peahens. Humans are the most complicated animals of all, shaped by upbringing and environment as well as by instinct, and it is not surprising that they should form powerful, exclusive or scarcely understood attachments to each other, prompted by countless conscious and unconscious physical and behavioural cues. In 1970, the sexologist Dorothy Tennov coined the term "limerance" for the state of being in love. According to Tennov, not everyone can become limerant (some

The Marriage of Cupid and Psyche (detail) by Raphael (1483–1520). To the ancient Greeks, love, like any other strong passion, was a form of madness, and madness was a curse of the gods. The god of violent love was Eros (Cupid). He himself became captivated by Psyche (soul), an allegory for the belief that love seeks out the spirit, not the body.

LOVE SICKNESS

Love sickness, an unrequited or unconsummated passion, so strong as to be incapacitating, is a feature of many Greek myths, most ironically that of the beautiful youth Narcissus, who wasted away staring besotted at his own reflection in a pool. The ancient Greeks had no real cure for love sickness, but later Oriental medical texts prescribed a no-nonsense programme of hot baths, music, erotic poetry and sex with someone other than the beloved. In the 11th century, Constantine the African translated some of these texts into Latin, as *The Viaticum*. His advice was especially valued by European knights, for whom love sickness for a woman represented unbearable subjection to a social inferior. What they found even more demeaning was that their own behaviour became "feminine" – passive, weak and emotional. Modern research suggests that love sickness may be related to the lack of a chemical, phenylethalamine, in the brain.

In Puccini's Madama Butterfly, *Cio-Cio-San kills herself for love of an American sailor.*

types of brain surgery can destroy the possibility), and those who can are limerant with only one person at a time. Sex is seldom the main focus for limerance, but at least the theoretical possibility of sexual contact has to exist.

Limerance is often described as existing only in the West, and is traced back to the romance tradition of the troubadours (see pp.84–5). It is true that many traditional cultures deprecate romantic love. The Mehinaku of the Amazon maintain that it serves as a magnet to evil spirits, while the Weyewa of Indonesia, who select and marry partners through elaborate systems of gift exchange, describe it as inhuman. Nevertheless, this does not mean that romantic love does not exist in these and other traditional societies, simply that these societies recognize the danger that sex and passion may pose to marriage, stability and order. Many peoples acknowledge the existence of romantic love, but try to ensure that it does not become the basis of marriage – far too important a social institution to be based on such a volatile foundation – and that it disrupts existing marriages as little as possible.

Most major religions, when they talk about the "love" of worshippers for their god or gods, are referring to such emotions of duty and respect due to a parent. Love for a god may also resemble adolescent hero worship: a desire to emulate rather than to possess. Passionate, at times romantic, love for a deity is typically restricted to religions whose gods have assumed human form. In the case of Hindu Krishna-worship, this love is endorsed by the god's own erotic behaviour when he was on earth (see p.69). The romantic love of Christ was, at various times, encouraged by the Church in an attempt to harness potentially unruly passion to the service of the established order. The writings of both the Christian ascetics and the love mystics (see pp.86–7) leave no doubt about the sexual underpinnings of much supposedly transcendent love.

Guilt and shame

In many religions, it is a commonplace that only the divine is real, and all else is illusion; but in all faiths, dread in the presence of the holy – what has been called the *mysterium tremendum et fascinans*, the awful and fascinating mystery – is equated to a sense of one's own unreality. The usual sceptical formula – while I may doubt everything else I cannot doubt my own existence – is short-circuited, and the self becomes the most immediate object of doubt. St Augustine, describing his "discovery of God as Truth", wrote: "Your light shone upon me in its brilliance, and I thrilled with love and dread alike ... I might more easily have doubted that I was alive than that Truth had being."

An existential, and not merely behavioural, shame seems inevitably to accompany a living sense of the sacred. In C.S. Lewis's retelling of an ancient Greek myth, Psyche tries to explain to her sister what it feels like to see a god, and admits to feeling "ashamed of being a mortal ... being, how shall I say it? ... insufficient." She feels, she says, as shy as a dream would feel, if it were seen walking about in the waking world.

Even in the absence of an immediate sense of the godhead, shame and guilt are necessary inventions of religion, insofar as religion is an attempt to explain the existence of suffering. To accept that the body is worthless, and an object of shame, is to accept that there is no reason why it should not suffer. Most mythologies teach that this imperfect existence is not what was intended by the gods – that it came about through human sin, such as Adam and Eve disobeying the word of Yahweh. The guilt for the original sin is transmitted through generations, and is paid for by their pain and death. Hunting and agrarian societies are intimately aware of the relationship between sex and death (see pp.12–15, 16–19), but often, especially as a body of religious thought becomes more abstract and diffused, the perception of this relationship becomes twisted, so that sex is seen as responsible for death. In many cultures, therefore, the introduction of sex into the world is

Adam and Eve Banished from Paradise *by Tommaso Masaccio (1401–28).*

PROMISCUITY

There is reason to believe that faithfulness to a limited number of partners, although a common social imperative, is not an innate human characteristic (see pp.10–11), and most societies reveal at least some ambivalence toward promiscuous behaviour. For example, the fictional seducer Don Juan first appeared in a Spanish play in 1630. In ensuing decades he became confused in popular legend with the real-life Don Miguel de Manara (1623–79), who reputedly slept with 1,003 women. Don Juan became something of a rogue folk-hero, even in a part of Europe where, and at a time when, a woman's honour was her highest possession. He achieves an apotheosis in Mozart's opera *Don Giovanni*, in which, defiant before heaven and propriety, he triumphantly chooses to descend to hell rather than repent.

Even in cultures where promiscuity is the norm, and plays an important role in maintaining the social fabric, there is a tension between actual behaviour and the folk myths that are supposed to govern it. The lore of the Amazonian Mehinaku tells of terrible revenges that may be enacted by jealous husbands, but at one time in the early 1980s, the thirty-seven adult Mehinaku were involved in eighty-eight extramarital affairs (out of a mathematically possible 150, excluding relationships forbidden by incest). Husbands are usually jealous only for the first few years of marriage, when the couple "prize each other's genitals", and any man who does make a fuss is scorned as an *itsalu*, or noisy kingfisher; wives who repeatedly reject extramarital advances are gossiped about as *teneju malu*, or worthless women.

The Death of Don Juan *by Charles Ricketts (1866–1931). Don Juan is confronted by the statue of the Commendatore, who will drag him down to hell.*

linked to the first ever death, and sex becomes the focus for the guilt that is responsible for human suffering.

The existence of sexual and bodily guilt in the devout does not explain its frequency in unbelievers, agnostics and the casually faithful. Freud, in his analyses of guilt and taboo, consciously struggled against metaphysical teachings about the absolute, and the possibility of a human relationship to it. Yet his own theories retain the *mysterium tremendum et fascinans*, as omnipotent, loving, terrifying parents (see p.107).

SHAME, GUILT AND DEBT

Attempts have been made to differentiate between "shame cultures", such as feudal Japan, in which fear of public scorn provides pressure to conform to social rules, and "guilt cultures", such as Protestant Europe, in which people are likely to act according to an inner conscience. Yet shame can be an internal sense of humiliation; and a large part of guilt-anxiety is a fear of being caught and shamed. The Danish *gaeld* means debt, and is related to the English *guilt*. Until recently, European peoples made little distinction between formal debts that had to be repaid, and personal obligations engendering a sense of guilt if they were not honoured.

Pain and the body

The act of voluntarily undergoing pain, or of inflicting pain upon oneself, can serve many different purposes. In a number of societies, and for much of the history of Christianity, self-flagellation or scourging has been a technique for driving away demons that have attached themselves to an individual. The pain endured in acts of voluntary suffering may be seen as a penance for sin, or as a form of sacrifice. Often – for example, in Christianity, early Jainism and Hinduism – pain is a way of experiencing, and therefore sharing, the suffering of a deity or saint. A gradually increasing, regularly applied source of discomfort may be used by an ascetic as a form of training, allowing the mind to become undistracted by a world that is considered illusory, or deceitful. Yet, in many religious movements the sudden and prolonged application of extreme pain is used as a way to bridge directly the gap between human and god.

The experience of pain is often described as leading to the attainment of such a mystical state by denying the existence of the body – by creating a feeling so intense that it must simply be fled from, the mind achieves an hallucinatory freedom, and can soar into other worlds. In many cases this is undoubtedly what happens. However, pain more usually emphasizes the body: it obsesses the mind and becomes the sole object of the senses. Everything else is forgotten, so that, far from denying the body, pain unites the body directly with the divine, by denying the world that lies between them. There may be, therefore, two separate physiological mechanisms of transcendence. This notion is analogous to the fact that, in parts of Tibet, shamans

are divided into two types: those whose ecstasies involve flying into the sky to meet the spirits, and those whom the spirits come to and possess. (Sexual transcendence, which is almost invariably described as a form of "embodying", or possession [see pp.54–9], probably works through the latter mechanism, using the intensity of internal sensations to make the world that stands as a barrier before the gods a little less real.)

In the same way that flagellation, or some similar process, is used in an attempt to unite the human spirit with the divine, it may also be used to unite human spirits with each other. In the West, a preoccupation with ecstasy through pain is usually classified as either sadism or masochism. Both terms were coined by Baron Richard von Krafft-Ebing (1840–1902), the former after the Marquis de Sade (1740–1814; see pp.98–9) and the latter after Leopold von Sacher-Masoch (1836–1905). However, de Sade enjoyed experiencing pain as much as he enjoyed inflicting it, and may be regarded as the archetypal sadomasochist. He believed that pleasure was a sign that people were acting in accordance not just with their own natures, but with the Nature that was the reason and driving force of the universe. Therefore all acts that give pleasure must be natural and right. De Sade considered that the goal of sexual intercourse was to produce physical changes in one's partner and oneself,

Donna flagellata e baccante danzante, detail from a Roman mural from the Villa dei Misteri, Pompeii (c.1st century BC). Flagellation often formed a part of the orgiastic festivals of the god Bacchus (see pp.54–9).

and noted that pain produces great physical changes, so that it is the most intense form of sexual feeling possible. In his wish for a totality of experience, de Sade sought to obliterate the differences between the sexes. In his stories, the roles of aggressor and victim cannot be experienced simultaneously, but are often alternated, a change signified by the passing over of a whip, an india-rubber dildo or some other obvious penis-substitute (see pp.98–9).

Sadomasochism – in its extreme forms – is clinically labelled a "perversion". However, the notion of what is or is not a perversion varies from culture

to culture, and from time to time within a single society – the American Psychiatric Association ceased labelling homosexuality as a mental illness as recently as 1974. The history of perversion as a classificatory concept is a brief one, and dates back to the 19th century, when psychologists and sexologists such as Krafft-Ebing and Havelock Ellis (1859–1939) began cataloguing what they thought of as deviations from the sexual norm. Gradually, the idea arose that perversion can be defined as a compulsive way of distracting attention from what would otherwise be a crippling sense of sexual anxiety. Fetishism is a typical perversion in this respect. It might have many causes, distributed throughout the individual's lifetime, but can ultimately be traced back to the long, crucial period when an infant is traumatically becoming aware of itself as a separate being, isolated from the world and from its parents. (Much of the behaviour that links sex with ideas of spirituality also addresses this anxiety; see pp.54–9.)

RIGHT Torso *(c.1930) by Man Ray. Leather or rubber clothing, along with some forms of slick, shiny cloth, are among the most popular fetish objects, probably because they retain, or even emphasize, the form of the body, while simultaneously conferring on it a glistening artificiality.*

Early researchers into fetishism stressed that it was predominantly a masculine condition. Freud called it a memorial to the castration complex: the infant child feels rejected from its parents' loving relationship and, because it jealously craves the sexual attention of both its parents (see pp.106–7), seeks to deny any knowledge of the distinctions between the sexes or the generations. The fetish object (which can be anything: there are documented obsessions with houseflies) is a version of the penis that the little boy imagines on his mother to quell his horror at discovering she has none of her own. Without this symbolic phallus, a woman is simply too different, her vagina too threatening (see pp.124–5). The body has to be mythologized, and made artificial, in order to be bearable.

TRAUMAS AND TRADITIONS

The term "fetish" was adopted by the psychiatric profession because there seemed to be a similarity between the phenomenon of sexual fetishism and the veneration accorded by African peoples to their supernatural fetish objects. Psychologists have a long and often ignoble history of seeking parallels between the workings of the Western

mind and the rituals of traditional peoples. There have been comparisons, for example, between initiatory scarification rites (see pp.36–9) and the Western phenomenon of "delicate self-cutting", practised (usually) by adolescent girls apparently in order to "let out" the anxieties and turbulent feelings caused by puberty. Critics of such theories hold that it is patronizing to compare traditional peoples with

emotionally disturbed Western adolescents. However, the more sensitive psychologists do not actually claim that rituals such as scarification are themselves pathological behaviour. Rather, they are ways of recognizing and making theatre out of universal human anxieties – and the symptoms of those anxieties – so that they may be acknowledged by society, and do not have to be endured alone by the individual.

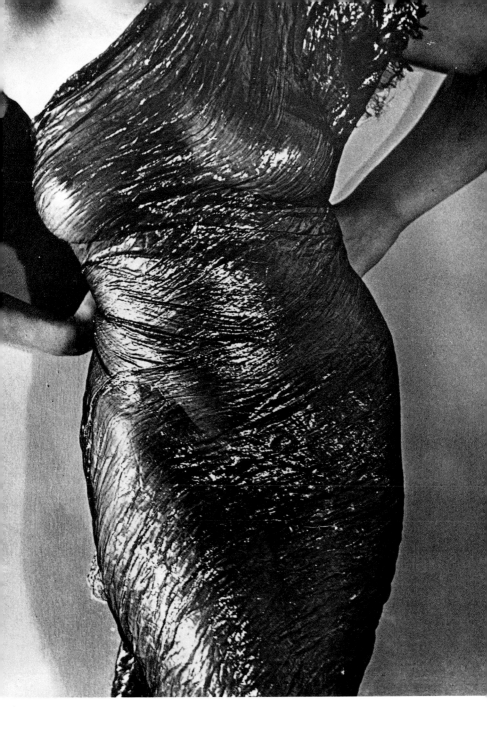

Incest and taboo

Some form of prohibition against incest is the nearest thing to a universal human taboo. Peoples such as the !Kung of southern Africa think of incest as "dangerous, like going up to a lion", and the Comanche of North America used to consider it neither a crime nor a sin, but simply impossible. However, there are numerous examples of incest being allowed, or even encouraged, in a culture. The most famous instances are the incestuous marriages of the royal houses of ancient Egypt and Inca Peru, in which brother and sister were required to continue the dynastic line. Half-sibling marriages were quite common in the ancient Near East and Europe, among the Persians, Greeks and Hebrews. In Bali, although half- and full-sibling marriages are forbidden, it is assumed that opposite sex twins have already been intimate in the womb, so they are allowed to marry as adults; by contrast, the Marshallese of the Pacific believe that such *in-utero* incest is cause

An alchemical image of the king and queen in incestuous union, from J.D. Mylius's Anatomia Auri *(1628).*

to kill the male twin. Other peoples, such as the Lamet of Asia, define kinship socially rather than by blood, and allow sibling marriage if the boy and girl have been raised in different households.

Sex between a father and daughter is more rarely sanctioned in any society, but is, in practice, the most frequent form of incest. A survey in the United States in the mid-1980s concluded that ten to fourteen per cent of under-eighteen-year-olds had experienced some form of incestuous attention, and that most were girls and young women abused by their fathers or stepfathers.

The rarest matings of all are between mother and son. Travellers' tales relate examples of this union worldwide, but there are probably only two plausible institutionalized examples. The Kubeo of South America require a boy to sleep with his mother to mark the beginning of his official sex life (although marriage between them is forbidden), and

---

NECROPHILIA

Death and decay inspire such horror in most people that they are surrounded by some of the fiercest taboos. The Pukapukan of Polynesia forbid even looking at a corpse, but consider it understandable if the cousin of a dead person is driven by grief to ravish the body. The East African Luo consider a young girl who died a virgin to have a dangerous ghost, and practise a ritual necrophilia to pacify it, calling on a stranger to deflower the corpse.

Taboos change over time. The Bellacoola of British Columbia now forbid the previously accepted tradition of a man copulating with the corpse of his wife as a sign of his grief.

Despite his extensive researches, the 20th-century Western sexologist Alfred Kinsey never met anyone whom he regarded as a true necrophile, and although corpses play a role in some Tantric rites (see p.147), the only traditional people reported as seeking out dead bodies purely for sexual pleasure are the Kainantu of New Guinea.

an east African Tutsi cure for impotence on the marriage night involves the man sleeping with his mother.

But even those societies that selectively sanction breaches of the incest taboo enforce it in all other cases. Taboo means both "sacred" and "unclean". A culture's permitted forms of incest usually fulfil a ritual or magical function, or, in the case of the Egyptian pharaohs, represent a claim to divinity (because gods are often portrayed in incestuous union; see pp.32–3, 62–3).

Most cultures regulate mating far beyond immediate kin. The Australian Aborigines have a complex and highly restrictive set of marriage regulations, based on the membership of clan or totem groups. Although the Bible does not prohibit cousin-marriage, and the

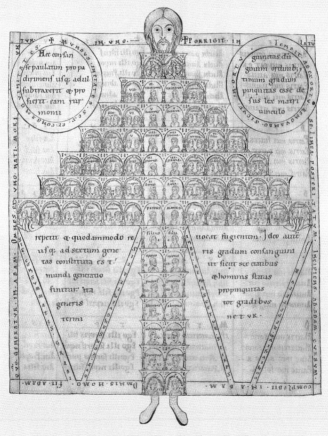

A consanguinity tree from a c.1150 edition of Isidore of Seville's Etymologiae, *showing the complex restrictions on marriage laid down by the medieval Church.*

Jews have allowed it throughout their history, in the 6th century Pope Gregory outlawed marriage between relatives out to a distance of third cousin. In AD731, Gregory III extended this sanction to sixth cousins, but by the Lateran Council of 1215 people were finding it so difficult to locate anyone whom they could marry that Innocent III had to revert to the first Gregory's ruling. Since the Council of Trent in 1563, Roman Catholics have been allowed to marry second cousins, and first cousins with special permission.

Despite their promiscuity, benobo chimps, like humans, observe the mother–son incest taboo.

There are several incest taboos that have nothing to do with blood kinship. For example, Muslims and Eastern Orthodox Christians may not marry anyone who was breast-fed by the same woman, and in parts of Catholic Latin America it is taboo to marry the children of one's godparents.

The anthropologists Edward Burnet Tylor (1832–1917) and Claude Lévi-Strauss (b.1908) have both suggested that there is no "anti-incest instinct". Lévi-Strauss has even speculated that primitive human groups would have preferred to inbreed, but that exogamous (outside the group) marriages were a necessary way to build kinships and political ties with other groups. Anthropologists have generally rejected the idea that early humans avoided inbreeding on eugenic grounds: deformities or mutations would not have

shown up for generations, and would probably have been blamed on witchcraft or malign spirits. Sigmund Freud (see pp.106–7) suggested the incest taboo reflects a deep-seated guilt at some primal act of cannibalism, from the time when the young men of an early human group would have to kill (and eat) the dominant father in order to gain sexual access to his wives, who would also have been their mothers. He based his theory largely on the behaviour of Australian Aborigines, who divide themselves into totem groups, each with a totem animal regarded as the spiritual ancestor of that group. The animal is taboo to the members of its group, who must not normally hunt or even touch it. Yet the group is obliged to kill and eat its totem on certain ceremonial occasions.

However, it seems that there is a more basic instinct militating against incest than either ingrained political expediency or infantile guilt, an instinct shared with the higher primates (and, indeed, most mammals with long life-spans and high intelligence). For example, benobo chimps, which share ninety-nine per cent of their genetic make-up with humans, engage in frequent, promiscuous sexual activity: yet even among benobos, where most permutations are found, there is no sexual contact between mothers and sons. But among humans the prohibitive instinct is imperfect (as can be seen from the

MISTRESS OF THE SEA MAMMALS

Sedna was a young Inuit girl, whose father chopped off all her fingers and threw her, and her fingers, into the sea. Sedna's fingers became whales and seals, and now she lives at the bottom of the sea and has control over those mammals. Because the dirt from human sins sinks downward and tangles in her hair, and because, with no fingers, she cannot clean it for herself, she is especially sensitive to the breaking of taboo. When she has been too badly soiled by human sin she will often withhold game from the people so that they starve, until a shaman comes down to clean her. Nevertheless, some Inuit groups set aside special twenty-four-hour periods when men and women pair off in tabooed ways, as this is thought to entertain and please her.

large number of child abuse cases), and can only be a partial explanation for the rich complexity of incest taboos found among human societies.

Other taboos are more obviously cultural constructs – taught rather than inbuilt – such as the plethora of restrictions and injunctions that surround a people's notions of modesty. According to Freud, taboo is the most primitive form of conscience, and conscience is the internalized form of parental authority. Among the earliest parental instructions concerning modesty or correct behaviour are those against the child playing with his or her own genitals, or with the genitals of other little boys and girls. Such instructions can turn into personal taboos that are so deep-seated as to be neurotic. Among the Oceanian Tikopia, it is taboo for a

Penis sheaths, such as these worn by the Yali of New Guinea, fulfil important modesty taboos by covering the glans, although their extravagance seems to call attention to the genitals as a whole.

man to touch his own genitals or the genitals of his partner, and the woman has to guide his penis into her vagina during intercourse.

Even people who spend all their time naked have elaborate modesty taboos. Among the Kwoma of New Guinea, boys are beaten from an early age for looking at a woman's genitals, while girls are trained not to sit or bend so that they expose themselves. A woman who sees even a young boy with an erection in public is expected to beat his penis with a stick. As with many traditional peoples, the breaking of sexual or modesty taboos is held to create a general spiritual malaise that has an adverse effect on other areas of life, such as success in hunting (see box, left). Commonly, it is not an activity but its timing that is taboo. Sex is typically taboo during menstruation (see pp.124–5), and usually during breast-feeding and pregnancy; it may also be forbidden as bringing bad luck before battle, hunting trips or competitive games. A number of peoples forbid sex during daylight, for different reasons; the Zulu believe that it reduces humans to the level of dogs, the Bambara that it would produce albino babies.

Menstruation

Few societies consider menstrual blood to be beneficial, although in medieval Europe it was sometimes tried as a medicine for leprosy, and Louis XIV of France believed it to be an aphrodisiac. Menstrual blood plays an important part in some Tantric rituals (see pp.144–55). Among the Ainu of Japan, it is a good luck charm, bringing success in the hunt and ensuring wealth; and it is also used as a medicine for relieving aches and pains. Consequently there is no taboo on sexual intercourse during a woman's period, and any Ainu man who sees a drop of menstrual blood on the floor will smear it on his chest.

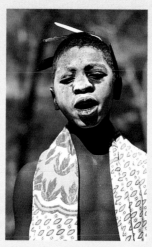

The initiation of a girl in Tanzania after her first menstruation, symbolizing her change in status from girl to woman.

In many parts of the world, however, it is considered dangerous for a man to sleep with a menstruating woman. If he does so he risks ritual contamination, impotence, a range of debilitating sicknesses or, in parts of North America, the immediate pregnancy of the woman. It may even be taboo to touch or see menstruating women. The Chukchi of Siberia consider their breath contaminating, and likely to make a man drown at sea. Jewish tradition forbids all contact during the menstrual period, and requires a woman to wash away her pollution afterward in a ritual bath-house.

Except for its stringent requirement that women wash after menstruating, Islam is less strict: on being told about Jewish prohibitions, the Prophet Muhammad is said to have replied, "Do everything [as normal] except sexual intercourse". Muhammad made his wife, Ayesha, wrap herself when she was menstruating, but afterward he shared a drinking cup with her, took a prayer mat from her hand, embraced her and lay in her lap. Yet local customs often prevail over religious orthodoxy: the Islamic Burusho of the Caucasus exile menstruating woman to a special hut, and at the end of her period, a Burusho woman has to wash with cow's urine (which is considered polluting in orthodox Islam), perhaps on the homeopathic principle that like cures like.

In some hunter-gatherer societies, where resources are scarce, taboos against menstruating women seem to have evolved as a form of population control. For example, the 19th-century Carrier people of British Columbia used to send girls into the wilderness as soon as they began menstruating. They had to remain in total seclusion for four years, and men avoided even the paths they walked on, as being dangerous and defiled. In general, however, menstruation taboos probably originated in the human tendency to turn any act that involves the spilling of blood into some form of sacrament ("taboo" simultaneously means "sacred" and "unclean"). A woman's ability to pour blood

DISGUISED MEANINGS

One of the roles of a fairy-tale is to prepare children subliminally for events in their lives that would otherwise prove upsetting or confusing. The opening lines of *Snow White* describe a queen, sewing at an ebony-framed window on a snowy winter's night, who pricks her finger and thinks her blood is so beautiful against the snow that she wishes for a child "as white as the snow, as red as the blood and as black as the wood". Soon afterward she conceives. On some level the child listening to the story absorbs the idea that some bleeding – at menstruation and later with the breaking of the hymen – is necessary for the making of babies, including herself. *The Sleeping Beauty* is also a menstrual fable. The thirteen fairies at the christening of the princess conform to the phases of the lunar calendar. The curse on the princess, as modified by one of the good fairies, is symbolic of the fact that, on reaching

An 1869 engraving from the Contes de Perrault *depicting Little Red Riding Hood with the wolf. The story warns about the dangerous, predatory males that are attracted by a recently discovered sexual maturity (symbolized by the colour red).*

puberty, she will spill blood, and have to endure a period of (sexual) inactivity before being "awakened" by her future husband.

regularly from her own body is awe-inspiring, and to some peoples, such as the Australian Arunta, enviable. The sight of a menstruating woman may also arouse male fears of a powerful, castrating *vagina dentata*, or vagina with teeth (see pp.37–8, 63).

Sometimes, this magical power of blood-spilling is specifically denied. The Christian faith was one of the first to diminish the importance – positive or negative – of menstruation. At the same time as it was turning the symbolic

The Eucharist symbolically depicted as the emblem of Christ's Passion, from the late 15th-century French Playfair Book of Hours.

drinking of the blood of Christ into its own central sacrament (the Eucharist), the Church taught that menstrual blood had no magical powers of pollution, and began to allow menstruating women to take part in services and to approach the altar. However, sex with a menstruating woman continued to be proscribed as unclean in penitential books. Older traditions prevail in Eastern Orthodoxy, which still does not permit menstruating women to take communion or to kiss holy pictures.

Masturbation

Active disapproval of masturbation has largely been based around the widespread concept of semen as an exhaustible resource, somehow connected by blood or spinal fluid to the brain (see pp.40–45). In ancient Chinese culture, masturbation among men was forbidden by medical books, as causing an irreparable loss of male essence, or yang (see pp.138–143); but it was permitted when a man had been deprived of female company for some time, when the flow of *ch'i* (energy) through his system might be clogged by a build-up of *pai-ching*, or devitalized semen. Chinese medicine was more concerned with nocturnal emissions, because these not only constituted a loss of essence, they were likely to be the work of a demon, draining the life from a man. Women were thought to have inexhaustible supplies of female essence, or yin, and were encouraged to masturbate; Chinese bedchamber books (see pp.132–7) describe a wide range of dildos and other toys for the relief of wives and concubines.

Similar ideas are the basis for most attacks on masturbation. The 18th-century French zealot S.A. Tissot described a man who had become insane through excessive masturbation, and another whose brain dried out so that "it could be heard rattling in his

Female masturbation has not been subject to as many rules as male, probably because it does not involve the spilling of seed. This 18th-century Indian painting shows a woman applying a mixture of honey and ghee to her yoni.

head". Tissot's warnings of insanity and "psychic impotence" bred generations of hysterical anti-masturbation texts, gadgets and even operations, such as adolescent circumcision. Even young

An ancient Greek vase depicting satyrs masturbating as part of a Dionysian orgy. In the festivals of Dionysos, solitary sexual acts such as this were frequently turned into feats of drama and gymnastics, to entertain the other participants.

SEED AND TEARS

The creation myths of the Egyptians concentrate on male deities. Atum, originally a local god of Heliopolis, became identified with Ra, lord of the sun. His name comes from a root signifying both "not to be" and "to be complete". Before time, he existed in the bosom of Nu, the primordial ocean, or chaos (also male). One Egyptian creation myth tells how, when he rose from Nu, Atum created the world by masturbating: "I ... had union with my clenched hand. I joined myself in an embrace with my shadow, I poured seed into my mouth, I sent forth issue..." When he wept over his creation, human beings sprang from his tears.

girls, though in no danger of spilling their brain-matter by ejaculation, were throughout the 19th century often subjected to chastity belts, modified girdles and, in extreme cases, clitoridectomy.

A more subtle attack on masturbation came from the psychoanalyst Viktor Tausk in the early 20th century. He noted that habitual masturbators became cynical toward the opposite sex, having been spoiled by fantasy; the masturbator expects an almost religious salvation by some perfect being. Sigmund Freud defended Tausk's views, and held that "the question of when masturbation is harmful and when it is not cannot be answered in general terms". For Freud, anxiety concerning infantile masturbation was a possible root cause of ritual activity (see pp.106–7).

In most societies, attitudes to masturbation have probably varied more than attitudes to any other sexual act – both historically and at any one time among different individuals. The later Judaic texts are much more preoccupied with masturbation than are the earlier sacred books; one clerical authority makes it a capital offence. Masturbation is not mentioned in the catalogue of sins in the *Spiritual Exercises* (1548) of St Ignatius Loyola, founder of the Jesuits; but the Catholic philosopher and theologian St Thomas Aquinas (1225–74) reviled it as worse than fornication, being a waste of semen that should be stored, through celibacy, for one's own spiritual profit, or spent in procreation for the glory of God. Aquinas dismissed female masturbation as "mere feminine lewdness".

Yet nothing in the Bible directly condemns masturbation. The *New Catholic Encyclopaedia* of 1967 calls it a "serious sin that will keep one from heaven", but only quotes a verse stating that the "covetous" will never inherit the kingdom of God. In 1720, to remedy this biblical oversight, a Dutchman named Becker coined the term "onanism", but the appropriation of Onan's name to condemn masturbation was pure theological fraud. In the book of Genesis, Onan "spilled his seed on the ground" and was struck down by God – yet his sin was not masturbation but a refusal to "raise up his seed" and fulfil his duty to impregnate his brother's widow.

Sexual ills

AIDS (Acquired Immune Deficiency Syndrome) was first medically recognized in 1981. At first it was so strongly identified with homosexuality in the United States that its original name was GRID (Gay Related Immune Deficiency), and many early articles and books used the disease to stigmatize the homosexual body as itself a form of infection – morally and physically corrupt, and spreading through the healthy, heterosexual world.

The need to blame others for what eventually proves to be a universal, sexually transmitted disease dates back at least as far as the 15th century, when Columbus's sailors referred to syphilis as "Indian measles" (by contrast, the Turks called it "the Christian disease"). Despite the spread of AIDS through heterosexuals, drug-users and haemophiliacs, and the discovery that in Africa it is overwhelmingly a heterosexual condition, the disease is still most intimately associated with the gay community. This, together with the fact that AIDS touches on another Western taboo area, that of death and the public expression of grief, has provided the gay community with an unwanted but powerful identity. The

Names Project Quilt – probably the most famous example of this identification – was founded in San Francisco in 1987 by Cleve Jones as a collective expression of grief. Each fabric panel, dedicated by its maker to a friend or relative who had died of AIDS, measures 6ft (183cm) by 3ft (90cm) – the size of a grave – and the quilt now covers more than fifteen acres (six hectares) when fully opened. It places panels for gay men and women next to panels for haemophiliac children, African women and children and drug-users. In the

An aerial view of the Names Quilts in 1994, emphasizing the vast number of individuals that AIDS has touched.

The Vampire *by Edvard Munch (1863–1944)*.

VAMPIRES

Vampires have always combined symbolic elements of sexually transmitted disease with elements of the disease's carrier. The image has never been more resonant than in the time of AIDS, and the vampire has rarely been a more popular subject for art and storytelling. The vampire, in its lore, literature and films, has always been presented as a seductive (or at least erotically potent), predatory individual. It feeds by what Ernest Jones, an early disciple of Freud, called "an exhausting love embrace", which perversely combines the sucking characteristic of love with the biting of hate. It may suck blood from its victim, or force the victim to suck its own. The vampire is an outsider that is nevertheless capable of transforming others into its own form: its process of reproduction is swift, unthinking and viral. The vampire itself is a sensual infection, spread by the sharing of vital fluid.

words of one commentator: "None are elevated or ignored; all are recorded. En masse, the panels form a mosaic of memory ... rich in lessons and lives."

Through the quilt, and other forms of art and memorial, the gay community has appropriated the symbols of martyrdom to bind itself together at a time of loss and danger. This is similar to the approach of the early, persecuted Christians, and much AIDS symbolism has been borrowed from Christian art. However, this has brought the gay community into renewed conflict with many Christian groups.

The position of many fundamentalist Christians has been that AIDS is a punishment from God for declining moral standards. This claim, in various forms and in various cultures, has been made for every sexual disease. Some Cuban cults have a specific god of syphilis, who visits the disease upon a person by possessing his or her body. Accordingly, the cure for syphilis is exorcism.

The myths that grow up around sexually transmitted diseases are remarkably persistent, despite their demonstrable falsehood and obvious danger. A widespread belief is that sexual diseases can be cured by having sex with a virgin; this is held to be true of AIDS in parts of Africa, and of syphilis in Jamaica and rural Serbia. The Mangaians of Oceania believe that gonorrhoea results from breaking the taboo of having sex with a menstruating woman, and also that a man will not catch the disease if he avoids ejaculating. In the West, bogus statistics have been used to promote Hebrew Scripture (Old Testament) ideas of cleanliness, by claiming that circumcized men are relatively immune to the HIV infection that causes AIDS .

Techniques of Ecstasy

Taoism, which developed in China, and
Tantra, from northern India, are the two best
documented esoteric disciplines that involve
the conversion of sex into a vehicle for
personal transcendence. They share many
features, and their ideas can also be found in
Western traditions of sexual occultism. The
main texts of both schools are concerned (not
exclusively, in the case of Taoism) with how a
man can achieve a state of ecstasy that will
transform his mind/body, and as a necessary
component of that ecstasy also require him
to arouse a similar state in his female partner
or partners. Both disciplines advocate the
reabsorption of semen in the belief that it
becomes transmuted into a higher substance
which will in turn transmute the individual.
Both hold that the mind/body is a mirror of
the universe, and so it can be perfected until
it is identical with the ultimate reality underlying that universe. And both at some level
conceive of that reality as sexually polarized
between male and female principles.

It is impossible to know for sure, but it is
likely that early Tantra borrowed heavily
from Taoist principles (such as *coitus
reservatus*, or reserving the semen) that
were brought back from China to India by
Buddhist missionaries. By the 8th century AD,
the Buddhist version of Tantra had reached
China, and began in its turn to influence
Taoist thought.

*In Tantra, drugs are sometimes used as a way of achieving a
glimpse of the transcendence that can only be properly attained
through ritual sex; or, as in this 18th-century Indian painting,
they may be taken as an integral part of the sexual ritual.*

Bedchamber books

The "clouds and rain" position, with the woman below and the man on top – as shown in this 19th-century Chinese manuscript painting – was considered the most auspicious sexual position, achieving a balance between heaven and earth.

The ancient Chinese compiled the first detailed manuals of sexual practice and advice. The official Imperial history of the early Han dynasty (202BC–AD24) lists eight handbooks of sex in its bibliographic section, under the heading *Fang-chung*, The Art of the Bedchamber. These books no longer exist, but parts of them at least have survived as quotations in a Japanese medical text, the *I-shin-po*, compiled by Tamba Yasuyori, a Chinese physician living in Japan at the end of the 10th century.

The manuals are largely in the form of dialogues between sages, Taoist Immortals (usually divinized human beings, rather than gods) and wise women. One prominent character is Huang-tsi, the mythical Yellow Emperor who was thought to have lived some 3,000 years before the Han dynasty. The Yellow Emperor ascended to heaven as a Taoist Immortal, riding on the back of a dragon, partly because of his skill in distilling magical drugs, but largely because, in his life, he had intercourse with 1,200 women, after

THE *ANANGA RANGA*

In the millennium that passed between the 3rd–5th-century *Kama Sutra* and the 16th-century *Ananga Ranga*, opportunities for pre-marital and extra-marital sex dwindled, and child-marriage became commonplace. The *Ananga Ranga* was specifically written to tell one man or woman how to live a lifetime with only one sexual partner. Its profusion of rules, routines and prescriptions is matched by

A painting (c.1900) of the type that may have illustrated the Ananga Ranga.

their particularity. There are detailed descriptions of what actions a husband must perform on what parts of his wife's body – including the big toe – for each of the eight watches of day or night throughout the lunar calendar. Whereas the *Kama Sutra* was written for lovers, the *Ananga Ranga* was written for husbands, with the main purpose of alleviating boredom, and as such it can be considered the template for almost all subsequent sex guides.

The Island of Women *(c.1870)*, *a Japanese erotic scroll. The Japanese followed the Chinese tradition of recognizing the importance of female sexual satisfaction.*

being taught the arts of loving by three female initiators: the Plain Girl, the Dark Girl and the Elected Girl.

The early Chinese bedchamber books are unique among the ancient sex guides in placing as much emphasis on female as on male satisfaction. The Plain Girl instructs Huang-tsi in how to make a woman relaxed, how to court her and how to know when she desires him; she tells him of the "five desires" and the "ten movements" by which he will know that he is satisfying her. Nevertheless, the goal of providing the woman with pleasure was primarily to strengthen her spiritual essence in order that this in turn would strengthen the spiritual essence of the man. The purpose of the Chinese bedchamber books was stated by the scholar Liu Hsang

(77–6BC): "The point of this art is to prevent one's potency from dying by preserving one's vital power and nurturing the male essence. Then one's grey hairs will turn black again and new teeth will replace those that have fallen out. This art of sexual intercourse with a woman consists of restraining oneself so as not to ejaculate, thus making one's semen return and strengthen one's brain" (see pp.40–45). The later Taoist alchemists, preoccupied with preserving their strength, or essence, would refer to women as "the enemy" for causing a man to emit his semen.

The Dark Girl who instructed Huang-tsi was also credited with several ancient treatises on the arts of warfare; and the bedchamber books, too, often talk about sex in terms of a battle,

This Hindu ivory panel from India would probably have adorned a bed or a love-seat.

ILLUSTRATION AND INSTRUCTION

The Chinese poem "T'ung-sheng-ko", written c.AD100, contains the first reference to erotic pictures being used as a guide by a newly married couple. The poem indicates that illustrated versions of the bedchamber books already existed and suggests that erotic scrolls were a traditional part of a bride's trousseau. In Japan, which adopted and maintained many traditions that eventually became obsolete in China, scrolls containing erotic images were a normal part of the bridal trousseau even into the 19th century.

It is likely that the original *Kama Sutra* and *Ananga Ranga* were highly illustrated; and ornately bound "love books" may still be given as gifts at traditional Hindu weddings, in order to help the couple consummate their marriage. However, nowadays, such books will usually contain only blank pages inside, serving a symbolic rather than a practical function, to protect the young couple from embarrassment.

---

referring to the participants as adversaries. Elsewhere they read more like medical texts than essays in the art of love. Nonetheless, the language is rich in metaphor and allusion. The penis was the jade stalk, the jade object or the male vanguard; the vagina was the jade gate or cinnabar (a red mineral) hole; and the various (precisely anatomized) parts of the clitoris were the jade terrace, the grain seed, the dark garden, the god field and the lute strings.

The Taoist techniques for reserving semen resulted in protracted love-making sessions. This, together with the large number of partners that a married man with a harem might be expected to satisfy in one night, meant that sexual variations were vital for maintaining interest. In the *Hsuan-nu Ching* (Handbook of the Dark Girl), written before AD200, there were nine positions, with evocative, often poetic titles, ranging from "Cranes with Joined Necks" to "Rabbit Sucking its Hair". By the 7th century AD, the *Tung-hsuan-tzu* (see p.139) had expanded these to thirty positions, although twenty-six were only variations on the basic four: male superior (Close Union), female superior (Unicorn Horn), male and female side by side (Intimate Attachment) and entry from the rear (Sunning Fish). Nevertheless, the author of the *Tung-hsuan-tzu* is clear about the set of variations that he considers to be most auspicious: "Man and woman must move according to their cosmic orientation, the man should thrust from above and the woman receive below. If they unite in this way, it can be called heaven and earth in balance."

The *Kama Sutra*, written in India between the 3rd and 5th centuries AD and attributed to the sage Vatsyayana, combines the Taoist mechanics of sex found in the Chinese bedchamber books with the mechanics of seduction as expressed in the Roman poet Ovid's *Ars Amatoria* (Art of Love; see p.99). It may have borrowed from both sources, although the *Kama Sutra* places greater emphasis on love, as distinct from desire or passion, than do Ovid or the Chinese. Vatsyayana constantly interrupts his descriptions of sexual or seductive technique to point out that the rules do not apply to those in love, who need only be guided by their own instinct.

However, there is an abundance of rules for everyone else. The *Kama Sutra* is obsessed with classification. There are nine ways of moving the *linga* (penis) inside the *yoni* (vagina), eight stages of oral intercourse and eight kinds of love bite; four kinds of mild embrace and four that are extremely passionate; three kinds of kisses that a man can give to an

The sexual positions prescribed in the Kama Sutra *were not always penetrative, as shown in this tenderly erotic Indian miniature.*

innocent girl, and four angles from which he can attempt to give them. The *Kama Sutra* was perhaps most influential in its unprecedented concern with genital size. A man's *linga* would identify him as a hare, a bull or a horse, while the capacity of a woman's *yoni* would mark her out as a deer, a mare or a cow elephant. A bull was ideally matched with a mare, and a horse with an elephant. The sexual positions mentioned are generally more acrobatic than those used by the Taoists, and the sage Suvarnanabha is quoted as recommending that "they first be practised in the bath".

The "trick-horse" position is sometimes shown, as in this 18th-century painting from Rajasthan, performed between a rider and interlocked men and women. Here the rider is the god Krishna, and the horse is formed from his cowgirl lovers, stressing the spiritual aspect of love positions.

The *Kama Sutra* follows the trend in Chinese writing that likens sex to a battle or a quarrel. It recommends a whole repertoire of blows to different parts of the body, and classifies eight different kinds of scratch that can be left by the nails. Unlike the Chinese bedchamber books, the *Kama Sutra* equated spirituality with spontaneity, and then proceeded to catalogue sex in extraordinarily meticulous detail.

According to tradition, the author of the Kama Sutra, *Vatsyayana, remained a life-long celibate and ascetic. However, his work is written in praise of love, and of enjoyment "by the five senses". Early in the* Kama Sutra, *Vatsyayana faces the objection that sexual intercourse is practised even by animals and does not need such an elevated approach. Between men and women, Vatsyayana retorts, it requires thought and the application of proper means. The four sexual* bandhas, *or positions, shown here are instructive illustrations dating from the 19th century, demonstrating the ritualistic and almost sacred nature of the sexual act.*

Taoism

Taoism of some description existed as a system of folk wisdoms for centuries even before Lao Tzu is believed to have collected its principles in the *Tao-te Ching* in the 6th century BC. The Tao, or way, is the ultimate reality, impersonal and before all gods or heavens. It is expressed as energy, movement and constant change, in which balanced and harmonious opposites contin-

The Taoist symbol of the complementary opposites, yin and yang. Yin is the passive principle of the universe, associated with earth, dark and cold; yang, the active principle, is associated with heaven, light and heat.

ually unite and metamorphose into each other. These polar opposites are yin (female) and yang (male), and the flow of energy between and through them (*ch'i*) is considered the same as the life force that flows in the human body.

The philosophy of Taoism provides a way for the insignificant and vulne.able human to endure in this endless flux. In order to achieve longevity – even

immortality – Taoism prescribes the cultivation of harmony, moderation, flexibility and conservation. According to Lao Tzu, the Taoist aims "to know the male ... but to abide by the female". Death is the consequence of the separation of yin and yang. In the unborn child, the male and female principles have not been split: the foetus is full of *ch'i* and is considered deathless, like the Tao. The sage must try to recover this condition, for example by learning how to breathe like the foetus in the womb. Taoists are advised not to act (again, like unborn children) but to let the Tao act through them.

The sexual theories of Taoism arose out of ancient Chinese occult religion. They were not universally accepted by the philosophical Taoists until the 5th

A panel from a Chinese scroll (c.1850) of Mongol horsemen, entitled "The Lying Horse". The Mongols enthusiastically adopted Taoist erotic techniques after they conquered China in the second half of the 13th century.

HEALING RHYTHMS

The 7th-century AD physician Tung-hsuan believed that, just as the seasons and the movements of heaven and earth had their natural rhythms which facilitated the flow of yin and yang, so sexual intercourse had to establish similar rhythms in order to be effective. Of the sixteen chapters in his book, the *Tung-hsuan-tzu*, seven are devoted to the discussion of thrusting techniques.

According to Tung-hsuan, "a slow thrust should resemble the jerking movement of a carp toying with the hook; a swift thrust that of the flight of birds against the wind". He recommends that a man should vary the nature, duration and intervals of his thrusting and that he should not "cling to one style alone for reasons of laziness or convenience". Tung-hsuan then describes nine different types of thrust, including quickly alternated deep and shallow strokes, like a "sparrow picking the leftovers of rice in a mortar";

and rising and plunging like a "great sailing boat braving a gale".

Even more important than the nature of the thrusts was the way in which they were arranged. Nine of one type followed by nine of another, followed by nine of another, often up to a total of eighty-one, was a particularly common prescription. The basis of these sequences lies in ancient Chinese numerology, according to which, odd numbers are yang. Three, as the first odd number after one, is considered especially auspicious. Three squared (nine) is even more powerful and nine squared (eighty-one) is often referred to as "complete yang".

If these precepts were followed, sex became a form of medicine. According to the *Yü-fang-pi-chüeh* (Secret Prescriptions for the Bedchamber), written in or before the Sui dynasty (AD590–618), "male–femalism [sexual intercourse] has eight benefits and seven ills". The benefits include firming male semen, stopping female bleeding, and curing

"coldness of the jade gate [vagina]"; and each has its own formula. For example, in order to regulate menstrual flow, "the man lies down straight and has the woman transport her buttocks and kneel on top of him. He inserts his jade stalk extremely deeply, and she carries out a count of seven [sets of] nine thrusts ... If done seven times daily, she'll be cured in ten days."

The seven ills that may be caused by excessive intercourse include fatigue (known as "stopped air"), discordant veins and blood exhaustion. Perhaps surprisingly, the cure is more sex, but once again in special positions and according to ritual, numerological formulas.

This miniature hardwood box from 18th- or 19th-century China, with its exquisitely illustrated fold-out panels, depicts a number of the different sexual positions that a couple might engage in for both pleasurable and medicinal reasons. Illustrated panels of this type might have been given as wedding gifts.

TAOIST ALCHEMY

In their quest for longevity, Taoist physicians evolved two main schools: that of the "inner elixir", which advocated the conservation of bodily fluids and the use of breathing techniques (such as the foetus's supposed "womb breathing"); and that of the "outer elixir", which sought to distil a life-prolonging "gold-cinnabar pill" from a mixture of cinnabar, lead and mercury. These approaches were not mutually exclusive.

In the most famous Chinese alchemical text, the *Ts'an-tung-ch'i* (Pact of the Triple Equation), the Taoist Master Wei Po-yang (*c*.AD 150) stressed that alchemical experiments were an exact parallel to the sexual disciplines used for attaining immortality. The woman was the "vessel of transmutation", or crucible; her ova, or red vital essence, were the cinnabar; the man's white semen was the lead; and the sexual technique, with its system of thrusts and pauses, corresponded to the firing times of the mixture over the stove.

Taoist sages perform an alchemical experiment, in a manuscript from c.1478.

century AD, when Taoism was formulated as a religion. After this the theory became more sophisticated, and sexual exercises were listed as one of the main ways to come closer to the Tao (the foremost way continued to be meditation).

In the *Su-nu Ching* (Handbook of the Plain Girl; see pp.132–5), probably written in the 2nd or 3rd century AD, Su-nu sums up the Taoist attitude to sex: "All debility of man must be attributed to the faulty ways of loving … Woman is stronger in thought and constitution than man, as water is stronger than fire … Those who know the Tao of loving and harmonize the yin and yang are able to to blend the five joys into a heavenly pleasure."

For the Taoist, man's yang force is like fire – volatile and quickly spent – while the yin of the woman is like the water of a vast sea, slow to move, but inexhaustible. The Taoist sex guides, therefore, recommend that a man absorb the yin energy of as many women as possible – by arousing them to a state of orgasm, and stimulating the flow of saliva, milk and vaginal secretions – without at the same time losing any of his yang by emitting semen. Although the old texts emphasize the boundless yin of the woman, this unilateral absorption of energy can seem like a kind of sexual vampirism (see pp.129). Some Taoist alchemists thought that yin could be extracted artificially, especially from virgins, and conducted experiments which often resulted in the death of their subjects.

By contrast, Taoist sex guides were strict on the subject of how often a man could afford to ejaculate before risking a dangerous loss of vitality. Strongly built men aged between fifteen and twenty could emit semen twice a day, thin men once. Strongly built men of thirty could afford one emission a day, and the frequency diminished until a strong man of seventy might ejaculate once a month – although he was advised not to do so at all in winter, because the loss of yang then was a hundred times greater than in spring. The physician Tung-hsuan (see p.139) described how a man could avoid climax by closing his eyes and concentrating, while stretching his neck and back, pressing his tongue against the roof of his mouth and breathing deeply through his nose. For those without the necessary powers of concentration, one ancient bedchamber book describes a more direct method: "Quickly and firmly use the fore- and middle fingers of the left hand to put pressure on the spot between the scrotum and the anus, while breathing deeply and gnashing the teeth scores of times." The author declares that this will turn the semen upward to nourish the brain (the immediate physiological effect is to divert it to the bladder, from where it passes during urination). This technique of *coitus reservatus* (also adopted by Tantra; see pp.150–55) is said to have allowed a man the necessary stamina to make love to many women in a single evening.

Two ivory statues, dating from the 18th or 19th century. Although the Taoists placed great importance on technical aspects of love-making (above), they also emphasized the tenderness that should exist between the partners (below).

In Taoist thinking, the quality and the quantity of sex are inextricably linked. Around AD300, the philosopher Ko Hung (also known as Pao-p'u-Tzu, the Master Embracing Simplicity) wrote that "the more a man copulates, the greater will be the benefit he derives from the act ... Copulation with only one or two women suffices to bring about his untimely death." Ko Hung also recommended that a man have sex with at least ten women a night.

To the ancient Chinese Taoists, good sex was a form of medicine, curing dis-

eases of the body and the spirit. It could even confer immortality. When the mythical Yellow Emperor (see pp. 132–3) asked the Plain Girl about the benefits of copulation without ejaculating, she told him that a man who engaged in the sexual act once without emitting semen, his vital essence, would be strong. If he did it twice, his hearing and vision would improve. If three times, his diseases would disappear, if four times his soul would be at peace. Five times meant that his blood circulation would improve, six that his loins would become strong and seven that his buttocks and thighs would increase in power. If he made love eight times without ejaculating, his body would become immortal. On the ninth occasion he would achieve longevity and the tenth time he would be like an Immortal (a divinized human). Among the gullible, and to the disgust of Ko Hung, Taoist ritual sex was also believed to ward off bad luck and gain promotion for officials and greater profits for merchants.

The possibility of strengthening the vital force of the body and the mind through sex led to numerous waves of popular mass-mysticism. Some sects, by promoting communal sexual rites, excited their disciples to the point where they believed that they had become invulnerable, a delusion that prompted a number of political revolts throughout Chinese history.

One religious uprising that may have been, at least in part, sexually inspired was the Yellow Turban rebellion (AD 184–c.204) – named for the scarves the Taoist armies wore – which was a factor in ending the late Han dynasty (AD 25–220). The Yellow Turbans practised *ho-ch'i* – "uniting the male and female essence" – and the slogan of the Patriarch Chang Tao-ling, one of their saints, was *ho-ch'i-shih-tsui*, "sexual intercourse will gain absolution from all sins". A succession of boy emperors had led to a weak and corrupt government, at the same time that a fairly organized Taoist church was established. This

This 19th-century Chinese print shows a garden in which a man is making love to a courtesan, who is also playing a mandolin. Courtesans were expected to be educated and refined, able to entertain a man with other forms of occupation than sex; music and painting, for example, played an important role in the courtesan's repertoire. As a result, courtesans were often the best educated, most accomplished women in a society which otherwise taught women to do little more than raise children.

Couple seated with a plant *(1821) by Hokusai. Japanese art absorbed and retained many Chinese conventions, such as the depiction of kissing as an intimate part of love-making.*

KISSING

The old Western myth – perpetuated even by experienced sinologists in this century – that the Chinese are offended by the idea of kissing probably arises from their reluctance to kiss in public. In fact kissing was held to be almost as erotic as coitus, and therefore something only to be done in private.

The Taoist Master Wu-hsien described a woman's saliva as her "jade spring", flowing from two points under her tongue and "greatly beneficial" if drunk. The flow of both her saliva and her vaginal secretions could be enhanced by drinking the "white snow" from her nipples, a practice that Wu-hsien described as the "Libation of the Three Peaks". By this method alone, the minister Chang Ts'ang (b.275BC) was supposed to have lived for 180 years.

Fellatio was endorsed by the old Taoist authors so long as the man did not waste his semen by ejaculating. It was even considered mildly beneficial, because yin might be absorbed from the woman's saliva. By the same token, cunnilingus was both popular and highly recommended. Oral sex between women was endorsed by the Taoist formula, "Softness close to softness enhances yin".

church was led by a high priest called Chang Chüeh, a charismatic figure who, like the leaders of some 20th-century cults, was able to gather thousands of followers. When an epidemic swept the empire, Chang Chüeh gained a reputation for miracle cures, and, carried on a flood of popular feeling, attempted to overthrow the Han dynasty and found a Taoist empire. His armies were defeated, and in the process the generals who beat them became so strong that they overthrew the Han dynasty themselves.

There were many subsequent radical popular movements based on Taoist sexuality, especially in the province of Shantung, notoriously the home of sorcerers and magicians. Governments of all stamps ruthlessly destroyed such sects, generally on the grounds that they "offended against good morals". In 1852, hundreds of followers of a Taoist magician died when the fortress in which they were barricaded was torched by government forces. In 1950, the Chinese People's Republic suppressed a Taoist sect because its "shamelessly lustful leaders" held beauty contests and encouraged its members to indulge in promiscuous sexual intercourse by promising that this would grant them immortality and freedom from disease.

Tantric principles

Tantra is a Sanskrit word meaning "web" or "weaving", which is usually interpreted as "that which expands understanding". However, Tantra is notoriously difficult to define. There are so many different schools and sects that it is almost impossible to make a single statement about Tantra that will not be contradicted by one of them. Hinduism and Buddhism both have their own versions. The oldest complete Tantric texts, the *Tantras*, were written by Buddhists and date back to *c.*AD600, but slightly later accounts identify some Tantric elements in the Vedas, the oldest Hindu sacred works. Hindu tradition mentions sixty-four *Tantras*, but there are actually many more, each with its own coded, secret language, and its own ideas and rituals.

A theme found in all the different forms of Tantra is also expressed in Mahayana Buddhism: "*samsara* is *nirvana*". That is, the illusory, shifting, everyday world (*samsara*) is identical with the eternal and unchanging (enlightenment, or *nirvana*). Enlightenment is not achieved by denying the world, or oneself, but by seeing them as contained within, and merging with, the transcendental reality. As one text says, "one should raise oneself by means of that which causes one to fall".

Another common thread running through all the various sects is the idea of cosmic sexuality. Everything, the sensible world and the transcendental, is generated by the sexual play of the goddess, Shakti, as she is penetrated by the invisible, impassive figure of the god, Shiva. This primal couple are inseparable, and are, in a sense, one. They are often represented in Hindu iconography

An 18th–19th-century Tibetan statue of a god embracing his female counterpart, or shakti: *the Tantric embrace, designed to unify opposites (such as male/female, light/dark), symbolizes the indivisible nature of ultimate reality.*

as the hermaphrodite figure of Ardhanarishvara. The first act of creation, according to the 3,000-year-old Brihadaranyaka Upanishad, occurred when the self-originated seed of being realized that "he was alone: he did not enjoy: one alone does not enjoy: he desired a second, and became like a man and woman in close embrace". To the Tantrika, or Tantric adept, this act of creation is continuous: Shiva's desire endlessly takes the shape of his fluid female nature, making the world for him to enjoy as bliss, consciousness and being.

Since the universe is born of desire, Tantrikas, unlike orthodox Hindu *brahmins* (the Hindu priestly caste), do not try to moderate their own desire, but to redirect its energy. The sexual exertions of Shakti and Shiva do not generate the universe as a homogeneous mass, but in

The postures of Tantric ritual sex, one of which is shown in this late 18th- or early 19th-century Indian album painting, create subtle circuits for the energy currents of the body. These currents amplify and enhance each other until they begin to resemble the energy that passes through the divine couple (Shiva and Shakti, the male and female principles).

TANTRIC TEACHING

The *Tantras* are obscure texts, using a seemingly haphazard appropriation of apparently contradictory icons and symbols and employing codes to describe important parts of ritual; additionally, most of the *Tantras* make it clear that there are some things that cannot be written down at all. To become a true Tantrika, the novice has to seek out a guru – but, because of their outcast status and their iconoclasm, authentic gurus are hard to find and harder to persuade into taking on new pupils. The Tantra of controversial New Age gurus such as the late Rajneesh Bhagwan bears only a passing resemblance to the true Tantra.

Tantric elements, real or imagined, have been imported into the West through many channels, including the occultism of Aleister Crowley (see pp.156–9) and the subsequent advocacy of Crowley's one-time secretary, F.I. Regardie, who went on to practise alternative medicine in California. The British psychologist Alan Lowen has employed Tantra as a healing tool, by using intimate contact and a rush of sexual energy to make people regress to their earliest, infantile experiences of sexual desire for, and rejection by, their parents.

INITIATION

A 19th-century Tibetan gilded bronze statue of a dakini.

One of the oldest themes in Tantra is the idea that a novice can be "charged" with divinity through intercourse with an adept of the opposite sex. Many rituals involve the initiation of a new practitioner by a woman who transmits her potency to him, having herself been converted into a vessel of the divine by engaging in sexual intercourse with one or more gurus.

Buddhist Tantra lays a special stress on this process of initiation: women with the power to create new male Tantrikas are called *dakinis*, and in recent Tibetan literature have become fantasy figures known as *kha-do-mas*, or sky-goers. Ancient Tibetan Buddhist texts describe how Padmasambhava, who brought Buddhism to Tibet, gained his power by raping a *dakini* in her home in a cemetery, then meditating in eight other cremation grounds. In Tibet and Nepal, it is still common practice for a (male) guru to place a statue of a *dakini* so that it straddles the lap of a (male) initiate as an act of symbolic, empowering intercourse.

successively less subtle halos of energy spreading out around the couple. According to Tantra, the human body and the cosmos are essentially the same thing, seen from different viewpoints. By a process of psychosomatic training (*sadhana*), the Tantrika tries to attune his or her own mind/body to progressively higher levels of this cosmic energy, until eventually he or she may become identical with the original double-sexed deity (see pp.32–3). The process involves activating the energy of the opposite sex in one's own body, by ritualized sexual intercourse. So-called right-hand path Tantra teaches that these sexual practices need not, and indeed should not, be performed bodily. They may be sublimated by meditation and performed only in the mind. They may even be performed purely metaphorically, in the form of one of the many alternative Tantric techniques that include the recitation of spells and words of power (*mantras*, see p.153). Left-hand path Tantra, conversely, holds that this kind of sublimation – although an ideal to be aimed at – is only possible for one or two great adepts in each generation. For most practitioners, sexual intercourse is a literal re-enactment of the divine fusion of Shiva and Shakti, and provides the best opportunity to identify with them and share their bliss. Certain Buddhist texts, such as the *Subhasita-samgraha*, state explicitly that "Buddhahood abides in the female organ".

LEFT AND BELOW
The famous temples at Khajuraho in India, dating from the 10th and 11th centuries AD, are covered in carvings that depict sexual activities. Temple carvings showing intercourse are said to please the storm-god Indra, because they advertise the sexual play of Shiva and Shakti. In return, Indra sends the rains.

The Tantric ritual sex rite (*maithuna*) is often called *yoni-puja* (worship of the vagina), and Tantra is widely credited with preserving archaic forms of goddess worship and importing them into the male-centred rituals of orthodox Hinduism and Buddhism. However, like most textbooks on sacramental sex, the *Tantras* are largely addressed to men, who must awaken their inner feminine energy in order to become whole, hermaphroditic and divine. The emphasis on the goddess in Tantric thought and iconography may be doing no more than reflecting this bias. Nevertheless, the *Tantras* do at least acknowledge that a woman can attain transcenden-

tal bliss, as opposed to the more orthodox thinking of the time, which held that she would first have to be born at least once more, as a man.

Tantra was not just a philosophically revolutionary movement. Most of its early followers are thought to have come from the lower castes, and much of its practice is specifically designed to break caste barriers and taboos. In the majority of the religions, sects or cults that use or have used sex in their rituals, the procedures may be only incidentally shocking, and then only to the outsider who does not understand or perhaps disapproves of their purpose. Tantric ritual is shocking by design, and in some of its manifestations is most

THE GRAVEYARD

Tantrikas are often instructed to make their homes in graveyards. There, the bodies of the dead are supposed to be cremated, but they are usually imperfectly burned, and the still-rotting corpses attract dogs, vultures and other scavengers. The work of handling the corpses is considered to be defiling, and is only carried out by the very lowest in the caste system. Yet the cremation ground is the place where all the castes finally merge. As such it has a multiple significance for the Tantrika: it offers a vision of the impermanence of the world, a practice-ground on which to conquer his own disgust and outrage, a theatre from which to disgust and outrage others, and an ultimate justification of his decision to reject the divisions of society.

More importantly, it shows him another face of the goddess that he worships, and with whom he seeks to couple. The would-be Tantrika has to be able to see the goddess as Kali, the destroyer and hideous agent of time, even at the very moment that he is making love to her as Shakti. The Buddhist version of Kali, Lha-mo, is if anything even more horrifying than her Hindu counterpart: she is portrayed wearing the flayed skins of her enemies, and pregnant with an incestuously conceived child which she will also flay for its skin. Bengali and Tibetan Buddhists were

An 18th-century brass statue of the goddess Kali, penetrated by the alert yet passive corpse of Shiva. The Karpuradistotram *text states that this is the image the Tantrika should meditate upon when engaging in ritual sex.*

instructed to meditate on her while sitting inside a rotting corpse.

Both Buddhist and Hindu Tantrikas copulated among dead bodies as a form of multi-faceted sacrifice, one of the elements offered up being their own sense of abhorrence. Any ingredients that might increase the loathsomeness of the ritual were therefore eagerly incorporated. One Tantric text, the *Karpuradistotram*, claims: "O goddess Kali, he who on a Tuesday midnight, after uttering your *mantra*, makes you an offering in a cremation ground of just one pubic hair from his partner, pulled out by the root and wet with semen poured from his penis into her menstruating vagina, becomes a great poet, a lord of the world."

upsetting to the person undertaking it. Self-esteem and social pride are seen as the biggest obstacles to enlightenment, and practices such as copulating among corpses, or seeking out menstruating (and so taboo) low-caste women as sexual partners, are meant to emphasize to the disciple as much as to anyone else the extent to which he has stepped outside the social order. Such practices increase his isolation: the true devotee ends up as a scandalous outcast. As the Hindu ascetic tries to deny the world in order to concentrate on the immortal, so the Tantrika tries to deny convention in order to concentrate on the world, the better to realize and direct its sacredness.

THE VEHICLE OF SPONTANEITY

Most Tantra is characterized by elaborate, intensive ritual – mainly, although not exclusively, concerning sex. Some Tantric sects concentrate more on magic, while others specialize in the manipulation of sound through the use of *mantras* (ritual syllables, see p.153). Whatever the method, Tantric ritual is usually directed toward a specific form of enlightenment.

However, the Buddhist Sahajayana (Vehicle of Spontaneity) sect does not prescribe any particular spiritual goal, nor any means of achieving it. To the Sahajayana, the very search for a higher reality merely reinforces the illusion of being separated from that reality, when in fact the divine manifests itself in, and indeed is responsible for, every action that we take.

DEVATAS

The halos of energy created by the coupling of Shiva and Shakti are represented by male and female figures called *devatas*. The varying

An 18th-century Tibetan bronze statue of Lha-Mo, the terrible Buddhist devata, equivalent to the Hindu goddess Kali.

interpretations of these figures is one of the main divisions between Hindu and Buddhist Tantra, although the difference is more important to the Buddhists than to the Hindus.

To the Hindu, the *devatas*, as aspects of Shiva-Shakti, have a kind of reality. They represent the subdivided energy-self of the goddess. Each embodied *devata* is an invitation to the Tantrika to identify his own body with the corresponding level of cosmic energy. Hindu Tantra holds that, if the ritual is performed correctly, what one

worships, one becomes: and worship involves welcoming one or more *devatas* into appropriate icons, so that they can be meditated upon and emulated.

To the Buddhist, the *devatas* are spiritual but illusory beings, the form in which Buddhist thought temporarily projects its analysis of the nature of reality. The icons that represent them do not, during rituals, house the entities they depict, but act as storage places for energies that are projected into them by the worshipper. Whereas Hindu Tantrikas strive to identify with increasingly subtle forms of the original, undivided couple, Buddhist Tantrikas strive to overcome increasingly subtle abstractions of the world-illusion, in order to identify with the void.

This Indian gouache (c.1800) depicts Mahavidya Chinnamasta, the Goddess of Great Wisdom. Garlanded with skulls and standing on the copulating bodies of a god and his shakti, *Chinnamasta unites the images of sex and death – opposing but interconnected Tantric principles. Chinnamasta decapitates herself to nourish her devotees, who stand at her sides to collect her blood.*

Tantric practice

Maithuna, or ritual sex, is the concluding part of a long, five-part ceremony known as the "five Ms", or *pancamakara*. The preliminary stages involve taking *madya* (wine), *matsya* (fish), *mamsa* (meat) and *mudra* (parched grain). All these substances are thought to have aphrodisiac properties, and the first three are ordinarily forbidden to Hindus. As a consequence, the *pancamakara* is often cited as an example of Tantric shock techniques: the need to experience the highest possible ecstasy via the lowest possible means (see also p.147). This assessment is probably a relatively modern rationalization of behaviour whose original purpose was nothing more than pleasure (itself a legitimate Tantric goal). Between the 8th and 11th centuries, fish, wine and meat (especially pork) were regarded as luxuries. The five Ms ritual may well have been part of the Tantric process of blurring distinctions between the castes

WORSHIP AND SACRIFICE

The basis of Hindu religious ceremonial is *puja*, the offering of food, flowers, perfumes, ornaments, music – anything of real value to the giver – to a deity who is usually made visible in the form of an icon. The Tantrika who performs an act of *puja* is, unlike the ordinary Hindu worshipper, applying it to his own body: because Tantra equates the body with the cosmos, the Tantrika identifies himself with the icon, and so with the deity that resides there. One of the most widespread Hindu icons is the *linga*, or phallus, and a common Tantric practice is to perform *puja* to one's own erect penis. A long Tantric ceremony may involve many different *devatas* (see p.148) – inhabiting an equal number of different icons – at various stages throughout the ritual.

Animal sacrifice is not a usual part of Hindu worship, despite the fact that it is described in the Hindu sacred texts, the Vedas. However, in Tantric temples such as the Kalighat in Calcutta, animals are still sacrificed, and there are reports that some Tantric sects practised human sacrifice well into the 20th century. *Puja* can be seen as a descendant of the ancient Vedic sacrifices, and because a Tantrika applies the symbolism of *puja* to his own body, the sacrificial aspects of the various offerings and anointings involved in *puja* become more obvious and important than in orthodox Hinduism. So, when flowers, bells, cloth, incense and food are presented to an icon, the worshipper is actually sacrificing the senses of sight, hearing, touch, smell and taste, respectively, to the divine presence in the icon. The worshipper's entire sensual world is offered up in order to be transformed.

Ejaculation, which is normally avoided during ritual intercourse, is sanctioned if it is performed as a version of the Hindu sacrifice in which oil or butter is poured onto an altar fire. In the Tantric equivalent, the rubbing of the sexual organs ignites the metaphorical fire, which is the pleasure experienced; the woman is the goddess, her vagina is the altar and the ejaculate is the sacrificial oil.

A devotee performs linga-puja *by placing flowers on the form of the* linga *in the* yoni, *representing Shiva and Shakti, and the union of male and female.*

(see pp.147–8), but equally it may have simply provided the Tantrika with experiences normally available only to the wealthy. Ganja (cannabis) and datura may also be used as a prelude to *maithuna*, but merely to provide a tantalizing glimpse of the ecstasy that can only be reached by devout, concentrated ritual intercourse.

The *Tantras* emphasize the dangers of *maithuna*, and state that the practitioner must be a hero (*vira*), free of doubt, fear or lust. An especially heroic Tantrika might perform *maithuna* with up to 108 women in a single evening, although some of these he would do no more than touch. *Maithuna* is a ritual of transformation, and although it is expected to generate pleasure, and through this transcendental bliss, the pleasure must not be of the ego – when the man and woman embrace, they do so not as themselves, but as male and female deities. One text, the *Kaula-valinirnaya*, describes the *panca-makara* as the "five-fold Eucharist", and states that "all the men become Shivas, the women Devis [goddesses], the hog's flesh becomes Shiva, the wine Shakti [Shiva's female counterpart]".

Because the *Tantras* are written by and largely for men, a great deal of care is taken in defining an appropriate female partner. In this, as in most other things, the various texts disagree. Some maintain that *maithuna* should only be performed by married couples, and that the woman has to be properly initiated first. Others advocate seeking out a menstruating woman of the lowest possible caste, although even in this case elaborate ritual purifications must be carried out, which usually involve

One of the most common positions in Tantric sex has the woman wrapping herself around the man, as in this 18th-century painting depicting the Janukurpura, *or "knee-elbow", position.*

anointing parts of the woman's body with perfumed oils. The most deliberately outrageous prescription for *maithuna* is in the 18th-century *Yoga-Karnika*, in which the god Shiva declares: "One should place one's penis into the vagina of one's mother and one's slippers on one's father's head, while fondling one's sister's breasts and kissing her fair seat. He who does this, O great goddess, reaches the Abode of Extinction. He who worships, day and night, an actress, a female skull-bearer, a prostitute, a low-caste woman, a

The Shri Yantra is the archetypal yantra, *composed of nine interlocking triangles that symbolize the male and female divine energies.*

YANTRAS

Yantras are diagrammatic representations of the fields and lines of energy radiating out from the sexual play of the divine couple, Shiva and Shakti; a pattern of lines and colours that represents the cosmos. A *yantra* may be powder sprinkled on the floor; it may be carved in the face of a crystal, or on the end of a *linga*; it may be made of red copper, especially if it is intended to evoke female energies (red symbolizes the female, white the male elements in Tantric iconography); and the floor plans of Indian temples are often in the shape of *yantras*. Tantrikas meditate on a *yantra* in order to absorb its meaning internally, so that it may provide a map for their own psychosomatic transformations. Indeed, the *Tantras* often state that the best *yantra* is the human body.

washerman's wife, he verily becomes the blessed Shiva."

Maithuna is usually carried out in a circle of initiates, guided by a guru. It may incorporate meditation, yogic postures, the recitation of *mantras* (sacred syllables, see box opposite), the visualization of *yantras* (see box, above) and the invocation of whole series of deities or *devatas*. The partners should ideally remain immobile, and the man should not discharge his semen. If by accident he does, he smears it on his forehead in the region of the "third eye", which allows him to reabsorb at least some of its potency. The moment of orgasm is, in theory, lost in a much longer wave of ecstasy, which does not involve ejaculation. The woman, on the other hand, may experience a conventional orgasm, and is even encouraged to do so, as this is believed to release the *rajas*, the vaginal secretion generated by sexual excitement. In some Tantric schools, the

production of the *rajas* is even the main objective of *maithuna*: it is collected on a leaf and added to a bowl of water. After being ritually offered to the deity, it is drunk by the man. (This is a powerful echo of the sexual "vampirism" that is practised by the Taoist alchemists; see p.140.) Even if the *rajas* is not collected outside the body, it is considered that a true adept knows how to absorb it through his penis, a technique known as *vajroli-mudra*, which enriches his own hormone system. However, the principal exchange between the partners in most Tantric rituals is considered to be sexual energy.

Within the material human body, Tantra envisages a complex system of channels, or *nadis*, carrying energy from the transcendental cosmos that pours in through the crown of the head. This system is known as the subtle body, which re-radiates part of its accumulated energy to form the self-generated illu-

MANTRAS

The subtle movement or vibration of the goddess has many grosser forms, which include the *devatas* (see p.148), and sound waves. *Mantras* are syllables or groups of syllables that are thought to be variations on the fundamental energy-vibration pouring forth from the goddess. A *mantra* may concentrate parts of this energy in the form of an associated *devata*. The nearest sound to the fundamental cosmic vibration is the mantra *Om*, the syllable of creation and dissolution. In the great *mantra* "*Om mani padme hum*", *mani* means jewel, thunderbolt or male organ, *padme* means "in the lotus [vulva]", and *hum* is a syllable for the highest form of enlightenment, or the supreme Buddha of a sect. The *mantra* is a reflection of the sexual union at the beginning and end of all things, and, compared to most Tantric ritual, is a relatively abstract device for mobilizing and directing the worshipper's libidinous energy. This makes it an important part of Buddhist Tantra, because unlike the Hindu Tantrika, who wishes to experience the cosmic desire of Shiva and Shakti, the Buddhist must ultimately try to extinguish all desire.

sion that the material body experiences as the real world. (This radiation is thought of as waste, and is sometimes described as a rat, sucking at the Tantrika.) At various points along the centre of the material body, the inner radiations of the subtle body condense as *chakras* (wheels) or *padmas* (lotuses). Hindu Tantra basically identifies *chakras* at the base of the spine, the genitals, the navel, the heart, the throat, between the eyes and at the crown of the head (there are more in some classification systems). Buddhist Tantra locates *chakras* at the base of the spine, the navel, the throat and the crown of the head. Each *chakra* corresponds to a progressively higher state of awareness. Enlightenment, always described in male terms, is achieved by driving the energy that is coiled in the base of the spine (the female *kundalini* or serpent energy of the Hindus, or, for the Bud-

dhists, a personification of female energy such as a *dakini*) up through the different *chakras* to the crown of the head. To the Hindu, this is the seat of Shiva, and the *kundalini* is a manifestation of Shakti. By rousing the normally sleeping serpent, and causing it to shoot

An 18th-century painting from Rajasthan, showing Tantric sex depicted as a form of astral projection, in which multiple versions of the same couple form a complex, spiritual, copulating chain.

up through the body to the crown, the Tantrika re-creates the union of the god and goddess within himself.

Sexual dualism exists in the human subtle body as two nerve channels. The *ida* (Buddhist *lalana*), which is red, runs along the left of the spinal cord and represents female creative energy, the moon and, ultimately, the void and knowledge. The *pingala* (Buddhist *rasana*), which is grey, runs to the right of the spinal cord and is the male creative energy, corresponding to the sun and, ultimately, compassion and practicality. So long as these two channels remain distinct, the individual will continue to be trapped in the cycle of death and rebirth. To the Buddhist especially, the combining of these opposites within the body is seen as a way of cancelling them out, bringing the individual closer to the condition of the void.

The energy generated during real or imagined intercourse with a female partner, along with yogic techniques of breath control, stimulate the *kundalini* of the man, which blends with his unshed semen to produce *bindu* (translated semen). *Bindu*, like the foetus, is composed of the five elements – earth, water, fire, air and ether – and its forma-

Tantric intercourse involving a man and two women, as in this 18th-century painting from India, is regarded as potentially highly dangerous, as the erotic, occult energies are greatly magnified.

MUDRAS

Mudras are hand gestures that are thought to seal the body, so that its energies can be controlled. They also symbolize the transitions through various inner states. There are probably hundreds of *mudras*, but the *Mahanirva Tantra* lists the fifty-five that are in common use. Many are abstractions of movements that would have been made in ancient Vedic sacrifices, while others are taken from dance forms such as Kathakali.

tion in the body represents a form of conception. The *bindu* breaks away from the two sexual channels and generates a new, asexual central channel called *sushumna* (or *avadhutika*, the cleansed one) along which it travels to the higher *chakras*, and ultimately to the "lotus on the top of the head". There it unifies all the elements of which it is composed, as well as the different male and female aspects of the practitioner. The Tantrika, therefore, uses ritual sex to fuel a kind of internal alchemy, fusing spiritual energy with material (unshed) semen in order to unite the various elements of the self.

RIGHT *A visualization of the subtle body, from 17th-century Nepal. The* chakras *or energy centres are represented as lotuses in various colours and with differing numbers of petals. At the heart is the twelve-petalled* anahata chakra; *at the base of the throat is the* vishuddha chakra, *which has sixteen petals; the two-petalled lotus in the centre of the forehead is the* ajna chakra *or "third eye"; the* chakra *at the crown of the head is the highest energy centre, the thousand-petalled lotus where Shiva resides.*

BELOW *This 13th-century carving from India illustrates the* kundalini, *or serpent energy, which lies asleep in most people, after having created the world around them.*

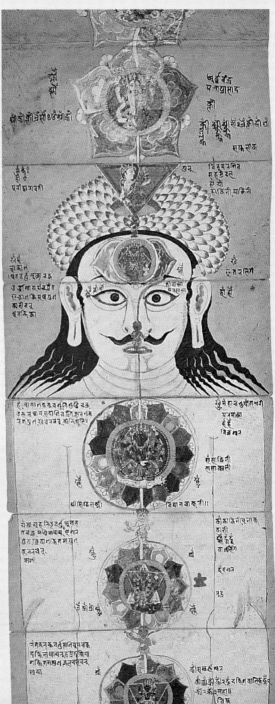

The new occult

After the end of the 17th century, the number of people who were persecuted for practising witchcraft in North America and Europe fell, while the number of people who actually practised it rose significantly. Although modern (that is, 19th- to 20th-century) occult rituals are frequently embroidered with fantasies (such as those of the 19th-century Abbé Boullan, who claimed to send his astral body through cloister walls to have sex with nuns), their principles are akin to those of the Cabbalists and Gnostics whose vocabulary they usually borrow (see pp.72, 75). The guiding idea is expressed in an 800-year-old Latin translation of the so-called *Emerald Tablet of Hermes Trismegistus*: "That which is above is like that which is below and that which is below is like that which is above, to achieve the wonders of one thing." Heaven, nature and humanity are part of a continuum, and so human emotions, drives and wishes can be used to change the universe. The more potent the emotion or drive, the more powerful the result. The sexual instincts, being among the most powerful of all, play a large part in practical magic.

The most influential 20th-century magician, Aleister Crowley (1875–1947), the "wickedest man in the world" and self-styled "Great Beast", had an insatiable sexual appetite. He borrowed the sex-rites of Tantra, Satanism and other esoteric disciplines, and invented more of his own. To almost all who met him, Crowley seems to have been a charismatic figure. He wore a "perfume of immortality" which he claimed made him irresistible to women (and horses, which whinnied after him when he

The 20th-century magician Aleister Crowley, who invented numerous black magic rituals, many attempting to harness the power of sex.

passed). After some of Crowley's creations were published in the journal *The Equinox* in 1912, he was approached by the Order of the Templars of the Orient, a German occult society specializing in sex magic, whose members thought that he had stolen their secrets. He subsequently joined the order, initially as a local leader, taking the title "Supreme and Holy King of Ireland, Iona, and all the Britains that are in the Sanctuary of the Gnosis".

One of Crowley's major inventions was the *Liber Samekh*, a ritual based on old Gnostic texts, in which the magician recites a long list of the names of powerful supernatural beings while masturbating himself to a climax. The ritual was also called the *Congressus cum Daemone*, or intercourse with the demon. It was explained by Crowley as a way of releasing, and knowing, the

THE PHILOSOPHER'S STONE

Modern occultists agree with Jung (see pp.108–9) in seeing the subject of the alchemist's experiments as being his or her own soul. The philosopher's stone, with its power to turn base metals into gold, is created simultaneously with a god-like being that the alchemist is forging within his or her own self. The process of forming the stone has either seven steps (corresponding to the biblical stages of creation described in the book of Genesis) or twelve (corresponding to the zodiac, and therefore the year, with its cycle of growth, death and rebirth). It basically involves a series of marriages, or conjunctions, between substances that are seen as opposites, such as mercury and sulphur, or body and soul.

In a typical formulation, based on the 15th-century account of the English alchemist George Ripley, the raw material (different alchemists began with different substances) must first be purged or fired (this is the action of the soul's discontent), then passed into solution (this is the dissolving away of the soul's habits and prejudices), before being separated into mercury and sulphur. This process is also the separation of spirit, or dispassionate intellect, and soul, or passionate nature; and the two, having been purified, must now be reunited. The remarriage of mercury and sulphur is referred to in alchemical literature as a form of incestuous copulation. The matter is now "killed", or heated until it putrefies to create the formless black "nigredo" (corresponding to the mock death of initiation ceremonies; see p.36), and then allowed to cool until the vapour that was driven off by the heat reunites with it, turning it white and bringing it back to life. The white stone, or new self, is now vaporized to purify it, and then recondensed. This is the first step in the true marriage of the spirit and the body, producing a spiritual body which is then married to the soul by fermentation. Such a marriage is described by Aleister Crowley as an ecstatic surrender to one's inner self, or as "the presence of Bacchus" (see pp.54–9). It leads directly to the philosopher's stone, or exaltation, when the alchemist, with soul, spirit and body in a state of rapturous harmony, achieves ecstatic union with the divine.

An alchemical image of Mercury and Venus making love, from the 1618 edition of Michael Maier's Atlanta Fugiens. Alchemical texts are rarely clear about whether they represent metaphors, or descriptions of concrete operations. However, following Taoist alchemy (see p.140) and yoga, modern Western alchemists tend to see alchemical recipes as allusions to breathing techniques and contortions that can be used to distil a "pill of immortality" within the body.

combined angel and demon that is the magician's unconscious. The recitation of the powerful names projects this liberated male sexual force into the universe, converting it from a metaphor for divine creative power into that power itself, so that, in the words of the *Liber Samekh*, "every Spirit ... and every Spell and Scourge of God, may be obedient unto me".

The defilement of innocence has always played a part in ritual black magic, but probably more as a manifesto than as a practice. Crowley said that the ideal sacrifice was "a male child of perfect innocence", and claimed that he had made just such a sacrifice about 150 times between 1912 and 1928. However, his diaries indicate that, like many other occultists, he used sacrifice as a metaphor for sexual intercourse. One of his followers explained that what is described as the sacrifice of a child is actually "the sacrifice of oneself spiritually" during the (not specifically paedophilic) sex act.

Most of the estimated 3,000 or more male and female witches in Britain (some estimates put the number of North American witches in the hundreds of thousands) claim that their rites are the remnants of a

continuous tradition of prehistoric mother-goddess worship, which is out in the open at last after centuries of persecution. However, most of the surviving witch-cults demonstrably came into existence after the publication of the esotericist Gerald Gardner's book *Witchcraft Today* in 1954. Many of their practices can be traced back only as far as Aleister Crowley, who was commissioned by Gardner to invent some witch-cult rituals in 1943–4. Gardner placed great emphasis on nudity, sexual intercourse and flagellation ("suffering in order to learn"), but the movement rapidly evolved out of his control. Splinter groups soon appeared, some of which did away with all sexual content – including nudity – in their rituals, while others exaggerated it, emphasizing the masochistic elements of Gardner's procedures. Almost every occult movement claims itself to be unique and authentic, but the continual cross-pollination of esoteric ideas – from Taoism to Tantra, from Gnosticism to Cabbalism – means that there is, inevitably, no such thing as an orthodoxy.

This mirror, in a frame designed to symbolize a yoni *(vulva), is used by a modern Wiccan (witchcraft) group in Toronto, Canada, updating the pagan image of the* yoni *as the source of all life.*

The Potter, *by the Canadian artist Chase. This modern witchcraft sculpture is symbolic of the regenerative principle: the form is vaginal, and the funerary urn is placed in the birth position – a clear link between birth, life and death.*

FAR LEFT AND LEFT *The Temperance and Lovers cards from the Tarot pack designed by A.E. Waite (*c.1910*).* BELOW *The Lovers card from a French Tarot pack based on designs published by Court de Gebelin in his* Le Monde Primitif *(1773–82).*

ASTROLOGY AND THE TAROT

Astrology and the Tarot are the elements of occultism that have penetrated most deeply into public consciousness. They are now popularly seen as simple forms of fortune-telling – a common, semi-legitimate pastime. But both have their basis in the same ritualistic roots as other forms of occultism, and both have often unexpected sexual elements to them.

Astrology follows the familiar occult pattern of dividing the world into male and female elements. The signs of the zodiac are alternately male and female (Aries is male, Taurus female, and so on); certain "planets", including the sun, are male, others, including the moon, are female. The moon is thought to sway everything outside the realm of intellect, including the animal instincts and the passions. The more a soul has evolved, the more immune it is to the influence of the moon and the more it is governed by the sun.

The Tarot has been used for centuries as a method of divination. The oldest known European cards are from a Tarot deck made for Charles VI of France in 1392. The three most popular modern Tarot packs were designed and interpreted by men (Aleister Crowley, A.E. Waite and Paul Case) who all at one time belonged to an occult organization called The Hermetic Order of the Golden Dawn, which flourished in Britain between 1887 and 1939. Certain cards are laden with erotic symbolism. For example, the Temperance card shows a figure pouring liquid from a silver cup (the moon) into a golden cup (the sun) – the pouring liquid may be interpreted as a spiritual orgasm, during which the soul ascends to a higher spiritual plane.

Tarot cards reverse the conventional symbolism of male and female: the Magician represents spirit, while the High Priestess represents the spirit's material aspects, such as the word and the law. In the Lovers card, which stands for celestial covenants and sabbaths as well as human love, the woman represents the attraction to the sensual life, which led to the fall from grace. She is not seen as a temptress, however, but as an agent of providence. Through her, and by combining with her, the man will complete himself and rise again.

Documentary Reference

Marriage customs and ceremonies

Throughout the world, a wedding is a form of treaty between families and a declaration of common interest more often than it is a declaration of mutual love. The family is the basis of most societies, and marriage is the covenant designed to guarantee the stability of the family. A wedding therefore becomes a public demonstration of this stability: symbolically, socially and economically. Even in materially poor areas, weddings are relatively extravagant affairs, because they must, at least partly, be displays of wealth – affirmations that the new family will be able to survive and prosper, reminders of the material ties to previous generations, and catalogues of any gifts or money that have been exchanged in order to cement the marriage.

The marriage feast fulfils both magical and practical roles. If there is no formal, written record of a wedding having taken place, the guests serve as witnesses to the reality of the union. The feast is also a type of fertility rite. In ancient Rome, a cake was broken over the head of the bride while she held three ears of wheat in her left hand, and a similar custom survived into medieval Britain. Now the cake is simply eaten. The Western custom of throwing rice or confetti is also a fertility charm – the favoured projectiles used to be ears of wheat or barley. This sort of sympathetic magic is not restricted to the feast or the post-wedding celebrations: in many religions, fertility spells are a traditional part of the ceremony, as when a Hindu bride and groom sprinkle rice or water over each other's head.

Other forms of magic or belief may play a part in wedding preparations. For example, most cultures exercise great care over the choice of wedding day, and Taoist, Buddhist and Hindu weddings are invariably planned after consultation with an astrologer to find an auspicious date. Another widespread custom, reported in rural Morocco, as well as among many sub-Saharan African peoples, and dating at least as far back as the ancient Spartans, is for the groom to dress in female clothing for the wedding ceremony, apparently to confuse any mischief-making evil spirits.

LEFT *This 19th-century painting shows a Chinese wedding ceremony. A wedding is usually, to some extent, a public display of a family's wealth; here, the participants are typically dressed in rich, fine silk robes.*

The religious status of a wedding varies from culture to culture, but even where the practical elements of the union are emphasized, and any spiritual dimension played down – as in much of traditional Africa – it is still customary for the couple to ask for blessings from the gods or ancestors. In a number of religions, such as Islam and some branches of Christianity, marriage may be conducted only in the sight of God, although in Christianity this was not always the case. Despite the efforts of the early Church to regulate the sex lives of its worshippers, marriage itself did not actually become a sacrament – requiring ecclesiastical participation – until the 13th century. Prior to this, all that was needed was for the couple to announce their intention of living together, and then to consummate the relationship.

A Buddhist wedding procession in Thailand. A Thai Buddhist wedding is more likely to take place in a hotel or a hall than in a temple, but the couple will usually go to a temple afterward to be blessed.

The union of husband and wife is symbolized in various ways. In Theravada Buddhism, a silk scarf is wrapped around the couple's hands and they eat from a silver bowl. A cord placed over a Hindu couple's shoulders has the same meaning, while in a Sikh wedding (and elsewhere, such as in parts of Meso-America), scarves worn by the bride and the groom are knotted together. In Judaism and Christianity, the union is represented by a ring, an archaic symbol of completeness. The earliest-known wedding rings, dating back to ancient Egypt, were made of iron. The Israelites, as far back as Moses and Aaron, used gold. In parts of Ireland until the 19th century, people who could not afford to buy a gold ring would borrow one, believing that otherwise the ceremony would not be valid. Because of the wedding ring's pagan origins, it has at times been banned from the wedding ceremonies of Quakers, Puritans and Mormons.

Apparently identical symbols can have radically different meanings worldwide. The white dress of the Western, Christian bride is a mark of purity. In some other cultures, notably China, white is the colour of mourning; in Japan, a bride's white dress signifies the ancient belief that, from the moment of her marriage, she is dead to her family. In the 18th century, this was emphasized by making a bonfire of the bride's childhood possessions immediately after the couple was named man and wife. In Taoist weddings, a bride is expected to cry in order to express her sadness at being taken from her family, and in many cultures the man must at least make a show of wresting the woman from her parents by force. The Western practice of carrying the bride across the threshold, which was known in ancient Rome, has been described as a symbolic form of abduction. However, it has also been claimed as an attempt to prevent the bride from striking her foot on the threshold, which would start the marriage with an evil omen.

Monogamy is the most common form of marriage, although it is actually insisted upon by less than a fifth of the world's peoples. Some societies arrange marriages between the living and the dead, among them the Mormons, who believe that only the married can be redeemed, and that dead unbelievers can be saved if a Mormon spouse is posthumously found for them. The ancient Persians had a similar custom. Marriage to trees, or to the spirit inside them, has also been common, and can still occasionally be found. Among such symbolic marriages, one of the strangest is the old North American Kwakiutl custom that a man could marry the arm or leg of the chief.

While marriage in one form or another may be the backbone of a society, most peoples recognize that an unstable, unhappy marriage is not worth preserving, and make some sort of provision for divorce. Of the great world religions, only traditional Christianity and Hinduism take the view that marriage is indissoluble.

This map shows the distribution of uncommon marriage types worldwide. Polyandry – a woman married to several men – is extremely rare. One version of it occurs among the Pahaarii of India, whose bride-prices (gifts from the groom to the bride's father) are so great that brothers will normally pool their resources to acquire a bride between them. Complex marriage involves every man being married to every woman in a community.

BROTHERS SHARING WIFE

MEN NOT BROTHERS SHARING WIFE

VILLAGE "WIFE"

GROUP MARRIAGE

COMPLEX MARRIAGE

TWIN BROTHERS SHARING WIFE

FATHER AND SON SHARING WIFE

MOTHER AND DAUGHTER SHARING HUSBAND

Love spells

Countless folklores describe methods by which a young man
or woman may learn the name, or see the face, of a future
spouse. The most common method is to provoke a
divinatory dream by the use of different herbs. An old
English spell to enable a woman to dream of her future
husband, performed on St Valentine's Day, involves her
taking two bay leaves, sprinkling them with rose-water and
laying them across her pillow in the evening. On going to
bed, she should put on a nightgown inside-out, and whisper:
"Good Valentine, be kind to me. In dreams let me my true
love see." If she then falls asleep quickly enough, she will
have a vision of the man she will marry. Butterdock seeds,
rosemary, thyme, hempseed, plantain, marjoram and
wormwood are only some of the herbs used to make
divination charms. However, the herb on its own is never
enough: it must be accompanied by the proper procedure.
Often, the ritual has to be performed on a certain day,
typically the day of the saint whose aid is being invoked.

All Hallows Eve (Hallowe'en) is another favourite time
for making divination charms. A particularly simple spell,
dating back at least as far as the 16th century in England
and Scotland, requires that young men and women go out
together on Hallowe'en with their eyes shut and each pull
up the first piece of kale they come to. Its shape and size,
whether big or little, straight or crooked, prophesies the
physique of the future husband or wife. If earth is attached
to the roots, the marriage is likely to be fortunate. The taste
of the *custoc*, or heart of the stem, indicates the temperament of the future mate, and his or her first name can be
learned by attaching the stem above the door to the house,
and then asking the name of the first person who enters.

*Simple talismans are commonly
used as love charms. This copper
disc is dedicated to Venus and
bears the glyph of the planet and
its Cabbalistic guardian spirit.
Other talismans may be struck
on metal or drawn on parch-
ment, and often have spells
written around the rim to
increase their efficacy.*

EARLY LOVE SPELLS

Potions and charms to make others fall in love are among
the oldest recorded forms of magic. Although paleolithic
rock paintings have been found that may have served as a
form of love magic, the first recorded love spell was used by
men in ancient Sumer. They mixed the milk and fat from
holy cows in a ceremonial green bowl, and sprinkled the
mixture onto the breast of a young girl, who was meant not
only to become sexually available but to follow the man who
had applied the spell. In much of the ancient Mediterranean
and Near East, it was assumed that the liver was the seat of
the passions (this belief is still current among the Tuareg;
see p.58), and the liver of a young person who was killed
while full of desire made a potent love philtre, as well as an

effective aphrodisiac (a substance taken in order to produce, heighten or sustain sexual excitement).

The ancient Greeks used a wide variety of animal parts and organs to make love potions, including calves' brains, wolves' tails, snakes' bones, the blood of doves and the feathers of screech-owls, as well as parts of human cadavers. The udder of a hyena, tied to the left arm, was believed to conjure the affection of whomever its wearer set eyes upon. Some of the potions were highly dangerous. The Romans, who adopted magic recipes wholesale from the Greeks, made the use of love potions an offence after a number of accidents in which people were rendered unconscious, such as the general Lucullus (*c.*117–58BC), or killed, as is said to have been the fate of the 1st-century BC poet Lucretius.

In the present day, Trobriand Islanders are encouraged from an early age to gain sexual self-knowledge. To the Trobrianders, magic is indivisible from the process of falling in love. Young men and women will woo a person with spells that not only make themselves more attractive, but also carry sweet, enticing dreams of themselves into the beloved's head. Trobriand Islanders greatly value grace and physical beauty, and use a number of magic spells to enhance their attractiveness on ceremonial occasions.

MAGICAL METHODS

Most love magic works by one of two principles: sympathy or contagion. The simplest sympathetic magic was probably a spell used by the ancient Greeks, when faced with someone who would not respond to their advances. They roasted images of wax, supposed to be the objects of their affection, over a low fire, believing that the people who were represented would correspondingly become warmed with love. The aim was to make the image soft but not to melt it, as this would break its sympathetic hold on the beloved.

The more common magical technique to make someone fall in love is to gain control over him or her by acquiring some intimate object of theirs, such as nail-clippings or hair. Alternatively, the beloved can be brought into contact with an intimate physical part of the lover, especially a bodily secretion such as sweat, semen or menstrual blood. This is the favoured method of the African-derived New World religions, such as voodoo and Santeria. One Santeria spell reveals the influence of modern North American culture on ancient, traditional systems of magic. It is a fast-food love potion: "Prepare a hamburger patty. Steep it in your own sweat. Serve it to the person desired."

This illustration, derived from a 2nd-century BC Greek vase, shows a female magician "drawing down the moon" in a magical recipe against unrequited love. An invocation to Hecate (a goddess of dark places, frequently associated with sorcery) is involved, and in Greek and Roman love poetry, the drawing down of the moon was the stock-in-trade of certain female witches. In recent times, the practice has been re-adopted by modern witch-cults.

The principle of contagious magic also underlies many European love spells. A popular spell in Scotland had the lover draw a circle on a wafer with blood from the ring-finger. The wafer was consecrated, and half of it eaten by the person casting the spell, the other half administered to the object of affection. This ceremony was to ensure not only that the beloved became receptive, but also that the passion of the lover did not wane. One of the more grotesque love recipes, the "dead strip", was used in parts of Ireland into the 19th century. A lovesick woman was advised to go to a graveyard at night and exhume a nine-day-old corpse: she had to tear a strip of its skin from head to foot, and contrive to tie it around the arm or leg of the man she loved while he slept, and remove it before he woke. As long as she kept the strip of skin in her possession, the man would love her.

THE SCOPE OF LOVE SPELLS

Not all sex magic is concerned with acquiring, or predicting the identity of, a lover. The Chinese bedchamber books (see pp.132–5) were full of magical medical advice. In addition to formulas for enlarging a man's jade stalk (penis), or shrink-ing the jade gate (vagina) of a woman who had become enlarged, there were cures for male impotence and for the pain experienced by women whose husbands enjoyed excessive intercourse with them. The Hausa of West Africa have several varieties of sex-related spells – alongside stan-dard love charms, they use sophisticated spells to prevent a philanderer's spouse from discovering that he or she has acquired a new lover. Although the Hausa practise their love magic enthusiastically, they are in no doubt as to its relative efficacy. One of their most popular charms involves the use of dried bats, but for as long as anyone can remember, there has been an associated proverb among the men: "Forget the bat magic, the real charm for getting a woman is money."

Love magic is found in some form almost everywhere, but it is perhaps less developed among peoples who are more direct in their sexual approach. The Lepcha of Sikkim (in Himalayan India) have a little love magic, but it is hardly ever used because sexual advances are rarely rejected. Love magic is completely unknown among the Tewa of North America and the Kaingáng of Brazil, the latter of whom believe that all individuals except small children are carelessly and spontaneously sexual. At the other extreme, some groups, such as the Romanies in Europe and the Cree in North America, are noted for their skill at weaving love charms, and are visited by surrounding communities.

A 16th-century hand-coloured woodcut from an illustrated herbal, showing the humanoid mandrake. Because of the resemblance that the forked mandrake root bears to the human form, in medieval times it was believed to possess both human and superhuman powers, and was often used in love magic.

SYMBOLIC STIMULANTS

One of the earliest recorded aphrodisiacs is powdered
crocodile penis, which was popular among the ancient
Egyptians. Many aphrodisiacs, ancient and modern, derive
their supposed powers less from their chemical constituents
than from the magic associated with their phallic shapes.
For example, stags' horn has been used as an aphrodisiac
throughout Europe, the knob on the bill of the king eider-
duck is a prized sexual stimulant among native groups in
Greenland, and rhino horn fetches high prices as a treat-
ment for impotence throughout Southeast Asia and China.

Spices are also often cited as aphrodisiacs, in the apparent
belief that the heat of their flavour in some way relates to the
heat of passion. Some aphrodisiacs are highly dangerous,
such as Spanish fly, which is made from the dried bodies of
cantharides beetles and is potentially lethal. Its consumption is still risked by some, because it can prolong erection
and produce a powerful tingling sensation in the genitals.

The Fang of Gabon are probably the people who use the
most aphrodisiacs, having more than 100 different types.
The majority are plants, but they include other, more
esoteric, materials, such as the teeth of chiefs, the bones of
albinos and the sex organs of a deceased mother-in-law.
Aphrodisiac festivals are occasionally held in order to renew
the sexual energy of a whole village.

There is no substance that is generally accepted by the
scientific community as an authentic, safe aphrodisiac,
despite extensive tests. There have, however, been some
tantalizing, though inconclusive, results, in the case of a few
plant extracts, including yohimbine (derived from the bark
of an African tree) and exsativa (an oat-extract originally
used as carp food in China). There is a long, and more convincing, record of anaphrodisiacs (which diminish desire)
used as aids by those who have embraced, or been forced
into, a life of celibacy. The Roman writer Pliny the Elder
notes that the Vestal Virgins used such drinks to help them
maintain their virtue, while an anaphrodisiac called *bhesajja*
has reportedly been used by Cambodian monks for centuries.

BIRTH CONTROL

Although attempts to regulate human fertility usually
involve the propitiation of the gods, many cultures have
evolved magical and medical-magical procedures to try to
control their reproductive powers. In 19th-century Cairo,
women who were anxious to have children evolved an urban

The white bryony – shown here in a woodcut from the Passau Herbal *of 1485 – is often used in place of the mandrake (see opposite) as a love charm, because its root can also suggest the human form.*

ritual that recalls ancient agricultural ceremonies, in
which it was explicitly acknowledged that life sprang
from death. At the time, criminals were executed by
decapitation in a part of the city called the Rumeyleh,
and before the corpse was buried it was placed on a
stone table to be washed. The water and blood drained
into a trough at the foot of the table, which was never
emptied. Women who wanted children passed seven
times over and under the table, and then washed their
faces in the stagnant liquid of the trough.

One of the most feared powers of the witch is her
ability to cause sterility. A common way of accom-
plishing this in medieval and Renaissance Europe was to tie
a knot in a piece of string. The French philosopher Jean
Bodin (1530–96) described a woman "well skilled in the
matter" who explained to him that there were "about fifty
modes of casting the knot, so as to affect either spouse: that
it might be devised, so as to operate for a day, for a year –
for ever". This belief was related to the Scottish custom that
all knots on the clothing of the bride and groom should be
loosened before the marriage ceremony. Magical girdles
might also be worn against witchcraft, as in Germany and
other parts of Europe. Such girdles also brought about
speedy deliveries, and ensured that any children born would
be brave if they were boys, and chaste if they were girls.

A "snake girdle", made of beaded leather and worn over
the navel, was used by some Plains Native Americans with
the opposite purpose: as a contraceptive charm. Such
charms are well documented, and often quite unexpected.
Women of ancient Rome would try to avert conception by
wearing a tube containing a cat's liver on the left foot.
Better-off women preferred a piece of a lioness's womb,
stored in a tube of ivory.

Herbs and other chemicals have an ancient history as
contraceptives. A vaginal bung incorporating some form of
dung, probably a symbol of death or decay, was used in
ancient Egypt, and has been recommended throughout the
Near and Middle East. In the New World, the Hopi used a
powder made from the root of the jack-in-the-pulpit plant,
and the Shoshoni an infusion of stone-seed roots. Such
substances are usually taken by women, although the Navajo
had some drugs (including an infusion of rag-leaf bahia)
that they claimed made both sexes sterile. Contraception
and abortion are among the few things for which the com-
pendious *Kama Sutra* does not contain recipes. The author,
the sage Vatsyayana, felt that either procedure disturbed the
natural symmetry of reincarnation, death and rebirth.

*A fertility charm from Egypt,
dating from the New Kingdom
(1539–1075 BC), an example
of sympathetic magic. Fertility
charms frequently depicted
couples making love – often
gods or animals noted for their
fecundity.*

Virtual reality

Modern computer research mirrors many of the concerns of the ancient mystics. Artificial intelligence attempts to create a simulacrum of the living mind from bits of inanimate matter, in much the same way that alchemists tried to make homunculi in their test tubes (see p.43). The original binary language, on which computer operations are based, was devised by the 17th-century German philosopher Gottfried Leibniz, who treated thought as merely the combination of signs, thus eliminating the gap between symbol and meaning that plagued theologians. Leibniz wanted to invent a universal form of expression, in which all conflicting ideas could be expressed and interrelated simultaneously, giving the thinker a god-like perspective. Such simultaneity is also the defining characteristic of cyberspace – a computer-generated "virtually real" universe made entirely of information.

Cyberspace can be apprehended in many ways. Helmets and earphones allow it to be experienced as sight and sound, special clothing can make it tactile. Ultimately, information from cyberspace might be transmitted by wires directly into the brain. A perception-disorder exists in which people feel sensations with the "wrong" set of senses, and similarly there need not be any preferential way of perceiving cyberspace: users could experience the colour of a noise, or learn what it feels like to touch – or make love to – a colour.

The term "dildonics" was originally used for machines that converted sound into tactile sensations. "Teledildonics" refers to machines that convert electronic signals in a similar way. They are usually gloves or suits with built-in air-bladders that apply varying amounts of pressure; more subtle methods use vibrating coils and special, shape-memorizing alloys, which twist and flex when a current is applied. It is already possible to immerse oneself totally in a virtual-reality universe, albeit a coarse, unsubtle one. As the technology improves it should become possible to tailor a personalized world as convincing as the real one.

The inhabitant of a virtual world will be able to exist in it as a third-person object that can be inspected with detachment, or as the "headless field of awareness" familiar from everyday experience. The cyberspace user will be able to possess another's virtual body, or allow his or her body to be virtually possessed; he or she will be able to change sex, or adopt a form of being in which the phrase "he or she" makes no sense; the user will be able to blend with other users, and experience the totality of their feelings. In short, all the goals and techniques of esoteric sexuality will be available through a computer interface, to a being who has, in his/her own version of the information universe, become divine.

Glossary

alchemy the forerunner of modern chemistry: a discipline that claimed to penetrate the mystery of life and transmute base metals into gold and silver

anaphrodisiac a substance used to diminish sexual desire

androgyne a person having both male and female sexual characteristics; *compare* bisexual

aphrodisiac a substance used to excite sexual desire

asceticism the practice of living by the principles of self-denial, austerity and abstinence from all worldly pleasures, usually for religious purposes

astral body a replica of the physical body, composed of spiritual plasma, that can be perceived by certain individuals in the form of an aura

Bacchant(e) the Roman equivalent of a Maenad: a (usually female) follower of Bacchus

bisexual a person who is sexually attracted to both men and women; *compare* androgyne, hermaphrodite

black mass a magical ceremony and inversion or parody of the Catholic Mass, exercised to mock the Christian God, and to worship Satan

Cabbala a body of mystical knowledge, originally Jewish, which became incorporated into Western occultism from about the 15th century AD

catamite a boy kept for homosexual sex; or the passive partner in sodomy

circumcision the act or rite of cutting off the foreskin of the penis

clitoris the erectile, hooded organ at the upper, external junction of the labia, or vaginal lips

clitoridectomy the surgical removal of the clitoris (so-called female circumcision) often as part of a religious rite

coitus sexual intercourse

coitus interruptus the practice of withdrawing the penis from the vagina before ejaculation

coitus reservatus the practice of delaying or avoiding orgasm during sexual intercourse

complex marriage every man being married to every woman in a community

cunnilingus oral stimulation of the vulva during sex

embryo an organism in its earliest stages of development, when the major organ systems and structures are being established

eugenics the practice of selective breeding in a human population designed to enhance desirable inherited characteristics

exorcism the religious act of persuading evil spirits to leave a person, place or object, by using command, ritual or prayer

familiar the spirit or demon companion of a witch

fellatio oral stimulation of the penis during sex

fetish an apparently ordinary or even worthless object which is nevertheless an object of veneration or worship, deriving from the 15th-century Portuguese *feiticos* (false), used to describe such objects among African peoples

flagellation beating, whipping or scourging, often as part of a religious discipline or as a sexual stimulus

foetus unborn offspring, in which the basic organ systems and structures are established

Hebrew Scriptures the Old Testament

hermaphrodite *see* androgyne; *compare* bisexual

HIV the name of the viral infection that attacks the human immune system, usually leading to the onset of AIDS

homunculus a microscopic, fully-formed human being, from which the foetus was formerly believed to have developed

incubus in folklore, a demon believed to have sex with sleeping women; *see* succubus

ithyphallic having an erect penis; perpetually aroused

libido sexual desire

limerance the state of romantic love, a term coined in 1970 by sexologist Dorothy Tennov

linga the phallus, or a stylized image of such, symbolic of the Hindu god Shiva, used in religious worship; *see also yoni*

Maenad a female follower of

the god Dionysos, Greek god of wine and orgiastic revelry; *see* Bacchante

Manichaeism a religious philosophy, deriving from the 3rd-century AD Persian prophet Mani, which portrayed Satan as coeternal with God, and taught that the flesh was inherently evil

necrophilia sexual intercourse with the dead

Oedipus complex according to Freud, a psychological state in which a (usually male) child subconsciously desires sex with his mother, creating a fear of, and a repressed wish to kill, the father

onanism masturbation; *coitus interruptus*

Oneida Community a utopian group founded in 1830 in Vermont, USA, composed of free-thinking Methodists who denounced monogamy, and practised group or complex marriage

parapsychology the study of mental phenomena outside the sphere of ordinary psychology, including telepathy and hypnosis

parturition childbirth

pederasty a sexual relationship between a man and a boy

polyandry marriage to more than one husband at the same time

polygamy marriage to more than one wife or husband at the same time

polygyny marriage to more than one wife at the same time

pornography the explicit description or depiction of sexual subjects or acts, intended to arouse an erotic rather than an aesthetic or emotional response

sacrament a religious act regarded as an outward sign of inward and spiritual grace; a thing or act of sacred or mysterious significance

Shakers a radical Quaker sect that flourished from around 1800 to the early 1900s, characterized by the practice of celibacy, common ownership of property, separation from the rest of the world and segregation of the sexes. Their name was drawn from their dances, in which men and women, on opposite sides of a hall, engaged in trance-inducing rituals of orgiastic shaking

shakti in Hinduism, the creative energy of the female, often personified in the form of the goddess Shakti, the counterpart of Shiva

shaman a spiritual specialist; a healer, seer or conductor of souls, who achieves contact with spirits while in an ecstatic state

sodomy anal intercourse

succubus in folklore, a female demon who has sex with sleeping men; *see* incubus

sympathetic magic a form of magic that aims to produce a large-scale effect through the performance of a ceremonial act that in some way resembles the desired

outcome: for example, the ceremonial pouring of water to induce rainfall

taboo an action or thing prohibited by convention, belief or threat of magical retribution, derived from the Polynesian *tabu*

theogony (stories of) the origin and descent of the gods

theosophy a philosophical system professing to achieve a knowledge of the divine through spiritual ecstasy or intuitive perception

totem an object or animal that is the hereditary symbol of an individual or clan, and is regarded as an object of worship

transvestite a person, especially a man, given to wearing the clothes of the opposite sex, often as a sexual stimulus or for ritual reasons

vulva a collective term for the external female genitalia

yang in Chinese philosophy, the male, active principle associated with heaven, light and heat, the complementary opposite of yin

yin in Chinese philosophy, the female, passive principle associated with earth, dark and cold, the complementary opposite of yang

yoni the name for the female genitalia, or a stylized image of such used in religious worship, particularly in Hinduism; *see also linga*

Bibliography

Ahlstrom, S.E. *A Religious History of the American People*, London, 1972

Andersen, J. *The Witch on the Wall*, Allen & Unwin, London, 1977

Arbuthnot, F.F. and Burton, R.F. *Ananga Ranga (Stage of the Bodiless One: the Hindu Art of Love)*, Medical Press, New York, 1964

Bailey, F.L. *Some Sex Beliefs and Practices in a Navaho Community*, The Museum, Cambridge, Mass., 1950

Balsdon, J.P.V.D. *Roman Women, Their History and Habits*, London, 1974

Bataille, G. *Eroticism*, Marion Boyars, London, 1990

Bataille, G. *The Story of the Eye*, Penguin, London, 1982

Bettelheim, B. *Symbolic Wounds: Puberty Rites and the Envious Male*, Collier Books, London, 1955

Beurdeley, M. (ed.) *The Clouds and the Rain: the Art of Love in China*, London, 1969

Bhattacharya Mahodaya, S.C.V. (trans. A. Avalon) *Tantratattva (Principles of Tantra)*, Ganesh & Co., Madras, 1916

Blaicklock, E.M. (ed.) *The Confessions of St Augustine*, Hodder & Stoughton, London, 1983

Boase, R. *The Origin and Meaning of Courtly Love*, Manchester, 1977

Bogoras, W. "The Chukchee", *Memoirs of the American Museum of Natural History* (Volume 11), New York, 1911

Bouhdiba, A. *Sexuality in Islam*, Routledge & Kegan Paul, London, 1985

Bowie, T. and Cornelia, V.C. *Studies in Erotic Art*, Basic Books, New York, 1970

Briffault, R. *The Mothers*, Allen & Unwin, London, 1931

Broch-Due, V., Rudie, I. and Bleie, T. (eds) *Carved Flesh Cast Selves: Gendered Symbols and Social Practices*, Berg, Oxford, 1993

Bryk, F. *Circumcision in Man and Woman: its History, Psychology and Ethnology*, American Ethnological Press, New York, 1934

Burton, R.F. (trans.) *The Kama Sutra of Vatsyayana*, Dutton, London, 1962

Burton, R.F. (trans.) *The Perfumed Garden of the Sheik Nefwazi*, G.P. Putnam's Sons, New York, 1964

Campbell, J. *The Masks of God* (3 volumes), Penguin, Harmondsworth, 1976

Campbell, J. *The Way of the Animal Powers*, Summerfield Press, London, 1983

Caplan, P. (ed.) *The Cultural Construction of Sexuality*, Tavistock, London, 1987

Cawte, J.E. "The Meaning of the Subincision of the Urethra to Australian Aborigines", *British Journal of Medical Psychology*, 39:245–253

Crapanzano, V. and Garrison, V. (eds) *Case Studies in Spirit Possession*, Wiley, London, 1977

Crowley, A. *Confessions*, Cape, London, 1969

Crowley, A. *Magick in Theory and Practice*, Dover, London, 1929

Czaja, M. *Gods of Myth and Stone*, Weatherhill, New York, 1974

David-Neel, L.E.A.M. *Initiations and Initiates in Tibet*, Rider & Co., London, 1931

Davis, W. *The Serpent and the Rainbow*, Fontana, London, 1987

Dörner, G. *Hormones and Brain Differentiation*, Elsevier, Amsterdam, 1976

Douglas, M. *Purity and Danger: An Analysis of Concepts of Pollution and Taboo*, Frederick A. Praeger, New York, 1966

Douglas, N. and Slinger, P. *Sexual Secrets: the Alchemy of Ecstasy*, Hutchinson, London, 1979

Dover, K.J. *Greek Homosexuality*, Harvard University Press, Cambridge, Mass., 1978

Edwardes, M. *Indian Temples and Palaces*, Hamlyn, London, 1969

Ellis, A. *The Folklore of Sex*, Charles Boni, New York, 1951

Ellis, A.B. *The Ewe-Speaking Peoples of the Slave Coast of West Africa, their Religion, Manners, Customs, Laws, Languages etc.*, Chapman and Hall, London, 1890

Eliade, M. *Birth and Rebirth: the Religious Meanings of Initiation in Human Culture*, Harper & Row, New York, 1965

Eliade, M. *The Two and the One*, Harvill Press, London, 1965

Eliade, M. (ed.) *The Encyclopaedia of Religion*, Macmillan, London, 1987

Epstein, L.M. *Marriage Laws in the Bible and the Talmud*, Harvard University Press, Cambridge, Mass., 1942

Epstein, L.M. *Sex Laws and Customs in Judaism*, Bloch, New York, 1948

Evans, T. and Evans, M. *Shunga: the Art of Love in Japan*, Paddington Press, London, 1975

Foucault, M. *The History of Sexuality: An Introduction*, Penguin, Harmondsworth, 1990

Foucault, M. *The History of Sexuality: the Uses of Pleasure*, Penguin, Harmondsworth, 1992

Frazer, J.G. *The Golden Bough*, Macmillan, London, 1922

Freud, S. *On Metapsychology: Including Beyond the Pleasure Principle, the Ego and the Id*, Penguin, Harmondsworth, 1982

Freud, S. *The Origins of Religion: Obsessive Actions and Religious Practices, Totem and Taboo, the Acquisition and Control of Fire, Moses and Monotheism*, Penguin, Harmondsworth, 1990

Fuller, J.O. *The Magical Dilemma of Victor Neuburg*, Mandrake, Oxford, 1990

Garber, M. *Vested Interests*, Routledge, London, 1992

Goldberg, B.Z. *The Sacred Fire: The Story of Sex in Religion*, Black Cat/Grove Press, New York, 1958

Goodland, R. *A Bibliography of Sex Rites and Customs*, G. Routledge & Sons, London, 1931

Gorer, G. *The Life and Ideas of the Marquis de Sade*, Owen, London, 1953

Govinder, Lama A. *Foundations of Tibetan Mysticism*, London, 1960

Gregersen, E. *The World of Human Sexuality*, Irvington, New York, 1994

Gregor, T. *Anxious Pleasures: the Sexual Lives of an Amazonian People*, University of Chicago Press, Chicago, 1985

Hepworth, B. *Confession: Studies in Deviance and Religion*, Routledge & Kegan Paul, London, 1982

Herdt, G.H. (ed.) *Ritualized Homosexuality in Melanesia*, University of California Press, Berkeley, 1984

Herdt, G.H. and Stephen, M. (eds) *The Religious Imagination in New Guinea*, Rutgers University Press, London, 1989

Jennings, H. *Cultus Arborum*, London, 1890

Jennings, H. *Phallic Miscellanies*, London, 1891

Jung C.G. (trans. R.F.C. Hull) *The Collected Works of C.G. Jung* (20 volumes), Routledge and Kegan Paul, London, 1953–1978

King, F. *Sexuality, Magic and Perversion*, Neville Spearman, London, 1971

Keller, E.F. *Reflections on Gender and Science*, Yale University Press, London, 1985

La Barre, W. *The Ghost Dance*, George Allen & Unwin, London, 1972

La Barre, W. *Muelos: A Stone Age Superstition About Sexuality*, Columbia University Press, New York, 1984

La Fontaine, J.S. *The Extent and Nature of Ritual Abuse*, HMSO, London, 1994

La Fontaine, J.S. *Initiation*, Penguin, Harmondsworth, 1985

Leach, E.R. *Genesis as Myth, and Other Essays*, Cape, London, 1969

Ly K'uan Yu *Taoist Yoga: Alchemy and Immortality*, Rider, London, 1970

Malinowski, B. *The Sexual Life of Savages in Northwestern Melanesia*, G. Routledge & Sons, London, 1932

Maybury-Lewis, D. *Millennium: Tribal Wisdom and the Modern World*, Penguin, Harmondsworth, 1992

McDannell, C. and Lang, B. *Heaven: A History*, Yale University Press, London, 1988

Mead, M. *Sex and Temperament in Three Primitive Societies*, Morrow, New York, 1935

Merkur, D. *Becoming Half Hidden: Shamanism and Initiation Among the Inuit*, Garland, London, 1992

Mernissi, F. *Beyond the Veil: Male-Female Dynamics in a Modern Muslim Society*, John Wiley and Sons, London, 1975

Meyer, J.J. *Sexual Life in Ancient India*, G. Routledge & Sons, London, 1930

Montagu, A. *Coming into Being Among the Australian Aborigines: A Study of the Procreative Beliefs of the Native Tribes of Australia*, Routledge and Kegan Paul, London, 1974

Muncy, R.L. *Sex and Marriage in Utopian Communities*, Indiana University Press, Bloomington, 1973

Nanda, S. *Neither Man nor Woman: the Hijras of India*, Wadsworth, Belmont, 1990

Nock, A.D. *Essays on Religion and the Ancient World*, Clarendon Press, Oxford, 1972

O'Flaherty, W.D. *Women, Androgynes and Other Mythical Beasts*, University of Chicago Press, Chicago, 1980

Onians, R.B. *The Origins of European Thought About the Mind, the Body etc.*, Arno Press, New York, 1973

Parrinder, G. *Sex in the World's Religions*, Sheldon Press, London, 1980

Pliny *Natural History* (10 volumes), Harvard University Press, Cambridge, Mass., 1940

Rachewiltz, B. de *Black Eros: Sexual Customs of Africa from Pre-History to the Present Day*, Allen & Unwin, London, 1964

Radcliffe-Brown, A.R. and Forde, D. (eds) *African Systems of Kinship and Marriage*, Oxford University Press, Oxford, 1950

Rasmussen, S.J. *Spirit Possession and Personhood Among the Kel Ewey Tuareg*, Cambridge University Press, Cambridge, 1995

Rawlinson, G. *The History of Herodotus* (2 volumes), Everyman, London, 1910

Rawson, P. *The Art of Tantra*, Thames and Hudson, London, 1973

Rawson, P. *Primitive Erotic Art*, Putnam, New York, 1973

Reich, W. *The Function of the Orgasm*, Panther, London, 1968

Reich, W. *Selected Writings*, Vision Press, London, 1961

Reichel-Dolmatov, G. *Amazonian Cosmos: the Sexual and Religious Symbolism of the Tukana Indians*, University of Chicago Press, Chicago, 1971

Reynolds, J.B. "Sex Morals and the Law in Ancient Egypt and Babylon", *Journal of the American Institute of Criminal Law and Criminology*, 5.1:20–31, May, 1914

Russell, B. *A History of Western Philosophy*, George Allen & Unwin, London, 1946

Scarry, E. *The Body in Pain*, Oxford University Press, Oxford, 1987

Schiebinger, L. *Nature's Body: Sexual Politics and the Making of Modern Science*, Harper Collins, London, 1993

Scott, G.R. *Curious Customs of Sex and Marriage*, Senate, London, 1953

Scott, G.R. *Phallic Worship*, Luxor Press, London, 1966

Shilts, R.M. *And the Band Played On: Politics, People and the AIDS Epidemic*, St Martin's, New York, 1987

Simons, G.L. *Sex and Superstition*, Barnes and Noble, New York, 1973

Spencer, W.B. and Gillen, F.J. *The Arunta: A Study of a Stone Age People*, Macmillan, London, 1927

Stephens, W.N. *A Cross-Cultural Study of Modesty and Obscenity*, Dalhousie University Press, Halifax, 1969

Summers, M. *The History of Witchcraft and Demonology*, Kegan Paul, London, 1926

Sur, A.K. *Sex and Marriage in India: An Ethno-Historical Survey*, Allied Publishers, Bombay, 1973

Tannahill, R. *Sex in History*, Hamish Hamilton, London, 1980

Taylor, G.R. *Sex in History*, Thames and Hudson, London, 1953

Tennov, D. *Love and Limerance: the Experience of Being in Love*, Stein and Day, New York, 1979

Ucko, P.J. "Penis Sheaths: A Comparative Study", *Proceedings of the Royal Anthropological Institute*, 1969

Ucko, P.J. and Rosenfeld, A. *Paleolithic Cave Art*, Weidenfeld and Nicholson, London, 1969

Unwin, J.D. *Sex and Culture*, Oxford University Press, Oxford, 1934

Valiente, D. *The Rebirth of Witchcraft*, Robert Hale, London, 1989

Van Gulik, R.H. *Sexual Life in Ancient China*, Brill, Leiden, 1961

Vitebsky, P. *The Shaman*, Macmillan, London, and Little, Brown, New York, 1995

Warner, M. *Alone of All Her Sex*, Picador, London, 1985

Warner, M. *Monuments and Maidens: the Allegory of the Female Form*, Picador, London, 1987

Wasson, R.G., Hofmann, A. and Ruck, C.A.P. *The Road to Eleusis: Unveiling the Secret of the Mysteries*, Harcourt Brace Jovanovich, London, 1978

Wehr, G. *The Mystical Marriage: Symbol and Meaning of the Human Experience*, The Aquarian Press, London, 1990

Weiner, A. *The Trobrianders of Papua New Guinea*, Holt Rhinehart and Winston, London, 1988

Westermarck, E. *A Short History of Marriage*, Humanities Press, New York, 1968

Westphal, M. *God, Guilt and Death*, Indiana University Press, Bloomington, 1984

Williams, W.L. *The Spirit and the Flesh: Sexual Diversity in American Indian Culture*, Beacon, Boston, 1986

Woolley, B. *Virtual Worlds*, Blackwell, Oxford, 1992

Young, S. *An Anthology of Sacred Texts by and about Women*, Pandora, London, 1993

Index

Page numbers indicate a reference in the main text. There may be references in captions or feature boxes on the same page. Page numbers in *italic* indicate a reference in an illustration caption only. Page numbers in **bold** indicate a reference in a feature box.

beneficial attributes 124
  symbolic male equivalents 38
menstruation 124–5
  conception soon after 67
  records kept in seraglios 66
  symbolized in fairy-tales **125**
  taboo on sex during 123, 129
Mercury (Greek god) *42*, *157*
Min (Egyptian harvest god) 64
modesty taboos 123, *123*
monkeys, symbols of sexual
  excitement **15**
monogamy 52, 76, 163
morality **99**
Mormons 162, 163
mudras **154**
Muhammad, Prophet 76, 124

N

Names Quilt 128–9, *128*
necrophilia **120**
nuns **58**, 67

O

obscene kiss *92*
Oedipus complex 38, 107, 108
Oedipus and the Sphinx (Ingres)
  106
oestrus cycle 10
onanism *see* masturbation
Oneida Community (Christian
  sect) *97*
onnagata (Kabuki theatre
  transvestite role) *53*
oral sex *46*, 47, 135, **143**
Order of the Templars of the
  Orient 156, **159**
orgasm therapy 111
orgasm *110*, 152
  key to mental health 110–11
orgiastic rituals
  cult of Cybele 38–9, 81
  cult of Dionysos 54–6, 57,
  116, *126*
  Feast of Fools 58
  voodoo **59**
  witches **93**
orgies *see* sacred orgies
orgone energy (radiation) 111,

111
original sin *78*, 82
Osiris 18, 62, **65**
ovaries 43, **44**

P

Padmasambhava *35*, 71
paedophilia 158
pain 36–7, *82*, 116–18, 158
Pan *49*, 55
Parvati (Indian goddess) *63*, 68
Paul (apostle) 74–5
pederasty 46–7, 48, 80, 85, 94
penis *see linga*; phallus
penis sheaths *123*
peoples
  Aborigines 23, 40–41, 121,
  122
  Ainu 124
  Akan **19**
  Aleut 51
  Alfur **41**
  Apache *39*, 51
  Arunta 37–8, 125
  Asmat **41**
  Athabascan 12
  Bambara 123
  Bantu 34
  Bantu Paia 23
  Beja *77*
  Bellacoola 44, **120**
  Bellonese 41
  Bemba **39**
  Blackfoot **19**, 20
  Burusho 124
  Canelos 22
  Carib **14**
  Carrier 124
  Cheyenne 51
  Chukchi 50–51, 124
  Cree **53**, 166
  Crow 51, **53**
  Desana 15
  Dogon *32*, 37
  Dyak **41**
  Ewe-speaking 25
  Fang 167
  Gebusi **57**
  Gisu **39**
  Hausa 166
  Hopi *39*, 168

  Hottentot *100*
  Ibo 25
  Ila 43
  Inuit *34*
  Kágaba 44
  Kainantu **120**
  Kaingáng 166
  Kayan 24
  Keraki 43, 47
  Khoikhoi (Hottentot) *100*
  Koniag 52
  Kubeo 120
  Kwakiutl 163
  Kwoma 123
  Lakota 51, 52
  Lamet 120
  Lepcha 166
  Luo **120**
  Mandan 13, **37**
  Mangaians 129
  Marind Anim 54, 56
  Marshallese 120
  Maya **15**, 46
  Mehinaku 113, **115**
  Nama (Hottentot) *100*
  Nasamonian 23
  Navajo 43, 51, 52, **53**, 168
  Nayar 10
  Ndembu 37
  Nyinbar 11
  Nyoro **37**
  Olo Nyadju 24
  Omaha 52
  Pahari 69, *163*
  Pina 51
  Pokot 37
  Pukapukan **120**
  Romany 10, 166
  Sambia 46
  Sebei people **39**
  Senufo *10*, *18*
  Shilluk **18**
  Shoshoni 168
  Sumerian 17, 164
  Tewa 166
  Tikopia **14**, 123
  Trobrianders 16, **22**, 40, 42,
  165
  Tshi-speaking 25
  Tuareg **58**, 164
  Turkana **44**, **115**
  Tutsi 121
  Waitata **14**, 23

Picture credits

The publisher thanks the photographers and organizations for their kind permission to reproduce the following photographs in this book.

Abbreviations
T top; **C** centre; **B** bottom; **L** left; **R** right

1 Bridgeman Art Library/Kunsthistorisches Museum, Vienna; **2–3** Bridgeman Art Library/Bibliothèque Nationale, Paris; **7** e.t. archive; **8–9** Biblioteca Apostolica Vaticana; **10R** Werner Forman Archive; **11** e.t. archive/Egyptian Museum, Cairo; **12** Bridgeman Art Library/Musée Conde, Chantilly; **13T** Ancient Art and Architecture Collection; **13B** Panos Pictures/David Reed; **14T** Bruce Coleman Ltd/Brian J. Coates; **14B** Ancient Art and Architecture Collection; **15** Werner Forman Archive; **16** e.t. archive/Ephesus Museum, Turkey; **17** The British Museum; **18T** Werner Forman Archive/Schindler Collection, Dallas Museum of Art; **18B** C.M. Dixon; **19** Stephen Trimble; **20** C.M. Dixon; **21** Bridgeman Art Library/Museo Diocesano, Cortona; **22** Panos Pictures/J.C. Callow; **23** Bridgeman Art Library/The British Library, London; **24** The British Museum; **25T** Werner Forman Archive; **25B** Bridgeman Art Library/Fitzwilliam Museum, University of Cambridge; **26T** Werner Forman Archive/Christie's, London, 1993; **26B** The Hutchison Library/Macintyre; **27** Bridgeman Art Library/Bible Society, London; **28–29** Gift of Denman Waldo Ross Collection/Courtesy of Museum of Fine Arts Boston; **30–31** The British Museum; **32** Werner Forman Archive/Private Collection, New York; **33T** Bridgeman Art Library/San Marco, Venice; **33B** Michael Holford; **34** Peter Furst; **35T** Science Photo Library/BSIP, S&I; **35B** Bridgeman Art Library/Oriental Museum, Durham University; **36** Panos Pictures/Steve Hilton Barber; **37** The Hutchison Library/Andre Singer; **38T** Ancient Art and Architecture Collection/Ronald Sheridan; **38B** Panos Pictures/Liba Taylor; **39** Stephen Trimble; **40** Bridgeman Art Library/Galleria Degli Uffizi, Florence; **41** ZEFA/Schafer; **42L** National Museum of Copenhagen/Kit Weiss; **43** Images Colour Library/Charles Walker Collection; **45** The Royal Library, Windsor; **46T** The Ashmolean Museum, Oxford; **46B** Werner Forman Archive/

Private Collection, London; **47** Werner Forman Archive; **48T** C.M. Dixon; **48B** The British Museum; **49** Ancient Art and Architecture Collection/Ronald Sheridan; **50** Bridgeman Art Library/Galleria Degli Uffizi, Florence; **51** Southwest Museum, Los Angeles; **52** Panos Pictures/Peter Barker; **53T** Artothek; **53B** The Hutchison Library/Macintyre; **54** Bridgeman Art Library/Giraudon; **55** C.M. Dixon; **56T** Werner Forman Achive; **56B** The British Museum; **57** The Hutchison Library/John Hatt; **58** e.t. archive; **59** Panos Pictures/Marc French; **60–61** Bridgeman Art Library/British Library, London; **62T** C.M. Dixon; **62B** Werner Forman Archive/The Egyptian Museum, Cairo; **63** Alistair Shearer; **64T** e.t. archive; **65T** Ancient Art and Architecture Collection; **65B** The Hutchison Library/Eric Laurie; **66** e.t. archive; **67** e.t. archive; **68** Trip/Dinodia Picture Agency; **69T** Bridgeman Art Library/Victoria & Albert Museum, London; **69B** Werner Forman Archive/De Young Museum, San Francisco; **70T** Werner Forman Archive/Collection Philip Goldman, London; **70B** Alistair Shearer; **71** Images Colour Library/The Charles Walker Collection; **72T** Bridgeman Art Library/British Library, London; **72B** Images Colour Library/The Charles Walker Collection; **73** Bridgeman Art Library/The Fine Art Society; **74** Bridgeman Art Library/Louvre, Paris; **75** Bridgeman Art Library/National Gallery, London; **76** Bridgeman Art Library/Fitzwilliam Museum; **77** The Hutchison Library/Sarah Errington; **78–79** Bridgeman Art Library/The British Library, London; **80T** Ancient Art and Architecture Collection/Ronald Sheridan; **80B** Staatliche Museen Zu Berlin; **81T** C.M. Dixon; **81B** C.M. Dixon; **82** Bridgeman Art Library/Vatican Museums & Galleries, Rome; **83** Bridgeman Art Library/Agnew & Sons; **84** Bridgeman Art Library/Giraudon; **85T** Bridgeman Art Library/Ron Miles Gallery; **85B** Michael Holford; **86** Bridgeman Art Library/Burghley House, Stamford, Lincolnshire; **87** Bridgeman Art Library/Santa Maria Della Vittoria, Rome; **88** The British Library, London; **89T** C.M. Dixon; **89B** Bridgeman Art Library/Museo Dell'Opera Del Duomo, Florence; **90** Bridgeman Art Library/Galleria Degli Uffizi, Florence; **92T** Fortean Picture Library; **92B**

Bridgeman Art Library/Prado, Madrid; **93** Mary Evans Picture Library; **94** Bridgeman Art Library/Hermitage, St Petersburg; **95T** Bridgeman Art Library/Galleria Dell'Accademia, Venice; **95B** "Male Nude" by František Drtikol (1921) courtesy Houk Friedman Gallery, New York; **96–7** Bridgeman Art Library/Johnny Van Haeften Gallery, London; **98T** Mary Evans Picture Library; **98B** Bridgeman Art Library/Victoria & Albert Museum; **99** Bridgeman Art Library/ British Library, London; **100** The British Museum; **101** Private Collection; **102** Superstock; **103** Mary Evans Picture Library; **106T** Bridgeman Art Library/Prado, Madrid; **106B** Mary Evans Picture Library; **106B** Bridgeman Art Library/Giraudon; **107** Michael Holford; **108** Ann Ronan at Image Select; **109T** Images Colour Library/The Charles Walker Collection; **109B** Bridgeman Art Library/Whitford & Hughes, London; **110** Noel Chanan & June Stanier; **111** Science Photo Library; **112** Bridgeman Art Library/Villa Farnesina; **113** Bridgeman Art Library/Private Collection; **114** Bridgeman Art Library/Brancacci Chapel, Santa Maria Del Carmine, Florence; **114** Bridgeman Art Library/ Tate Gallery, London; **117** Scala; **119** The Man Ray Estate; **120** Images Colour Library/The Charles Walker Collection; **121** Bayer Staatsbibliothek München; **122** Bruce Coleman Ltd/Rod Williams; **123** Panos Pictures/J.C. Callow; **124** The Hutchison Library; **125T** Mary Evans Picture Library; **125B** e.t. archive; **126T** Private Collection; **126B–127** The Museum of Fine Arts, Boston; **128** Rex Features; **129** Bridgeman Art Library/Christie's, London; **130–31** Bridgeman Art Library/Victor Lownes Collection; **132T** Private Collection; **132B** Trip/ Dinodia Picture Agency; **133** Bridgeman Art Library/Private Collection; **134** Werner Forman Archive/Private Collection; **135T** Trip/Dinodia Picture Agency; **135B** Private Collection; **136** Private Collection; **137T** Private Collection; **137TL, TR, B** Private Collection; **138B** Bridgeman Art Library/Private Collection; **139** Private Collection; **140** Alchemy & Chemistry/ Duncan Baird Publishers; **141T, B** Private Collection; **142** Private Collection; **143** Bridgeman Art Library/Private Collection; **144** C.M. Dixon; **145T** Werner Forman Archive/ Private Collection; **145B** Werner Forman Archive/ Philip Goldman Collection, London; **146C** The Hutchison Library/Carlos Freire; **146B** Alistair Shearer; **147** Ajit Mookerjee Collection, New Delhi/Jeff

Teasdale; **148** Werner Forman Archive/ Philip Goldman Collection; **149** Bridgeman Art Library; **150** The Hutchison Library/Patricio Goycolea; **151** Private Collection; **153** Private Collection; **154** Private Collection; **155L** Trip/Dinodia Picture Agency; **155R** Ajit Mookerjee Collection, New Delhi/Jeff Teasdale; **156** Mary Evans Picture Library; **157, 158L & R, 159L, R & C** Images Colour Library/The Charles Walker Collection; **160** e.t. archive/Victoria & Albert Museum; **162** The Hutchison Library/R. Ian Lloyd; **165** Fortean Picture Library; **166, 167** Images Colour Library/ The Charles Walker Collection; **168** Werner Forman Archive/Private Collection

Commissioned illustrations:
10L, 42R, 64B, 152TL, 164 Hugh Dixon
138T Ed Stewart

Every effort has been made to trace copyright holders. However, if there are any omissions we will be happy to rectify them in future editions.

To Kate, as promised